TRACING YOUR
FAMILY HISTORY
THROUGH THE CENSUS

FAMILY HISTORY FROM PEN & SWORD BOOKS

TRACING YOUR FAMILY HISTORY THROUGH THE CENSUS

A Guide for Family Historians

EMMA JOLLY

Pen & Sword
FAMILY HISTORY

First published in Great Britain in 2020 by
PEN AND SWORD FAMILY HISTORY
An imprint of
Pen & Sword Books Ltd
Yorkshire – Philadelphia

ISBN 978 1 52675 522 3

A CIP catalogue record for this book is available from the British Library.

Printed and bound in the UK by CPI Group (UK) Ltd, Croydon, CR0 4YY.

Pen & Sword Books Limited incorporates the imprints of Atlas, Archaeology, Aviation, Discovery, Family History, Fiction, History, Maritime, Military, Military Classics, Politics, Select, Transport, True Crime, Air World, Frontline Publishing, Leo Cooper, Remember When, Seaforth Publishing, The Praetorian Press, Wharncliffe Local History, Wharncliffe Transport, Wharncliffe True Crime and White Owl.

For a complete list of Pen & Sword titles please contact

PEN & SWORD BOOKS LIMITED
47 Church Street, Barnsley, South Yorkshire, S70 2AS, England
E-mail: enquiries@pen-and-sword.co.uk
Website: www.pen-and-sword.co.uk

Or

PEN AND SWORD BOOKS
1950 Lawrence Rd, Havertown, PA 19083, USA
E-mail: Uspen-and-sword@casematepublishers.com
Website: www.penandswordbooks.com

CONTENTS

ACKNOWLEDGEMENTS

I would like to thank Pen and Sword for their support with this second edition, especially Amy Jordan, Simon Fowler, Rupert Harding, and to Gaynor Haliday for her careful proof-reading.

Chapter 1

HISTORY OF THE CENSUS

Family historians have been using census records for over forty years. Often referred to as 'genealogy's most useful resource', the census became central to popular family history when searchable records were placed online in 2002. Before this, genealogists and other researchers had to search painstakingly through reels of microfilm to find their ancestors. Now transcriptions and images of the 1841–1911 censuses can be explored from the comfort of a home computer or at a local library. However, the census was never intended for the use of family historians. Some censuses have been destroyed deliberately over the years, while others have been damaged in war or through the damp and decay of poor storage. Where censuses have survived, it is often due to a chance event or the intervention of an official concerned with demographic, socio-economic or political factors. Censuses, in some form, date from early history, but family historians are most concerned with those created in the nineteenth and early twentieth centuries. This book will explore these, and look at how family historians can best use them for their research.

What is a Census?

According to the *Oxford New Shorter English Dictionary*, a census is defined as:

> *n. & v.* E17. [L, f, *censere* assess: cf. CENSE *n.*] **A** *n.* † **1** A tax, a tribute; *esp.* a poll tax. E17–M19. **2** *Hist.* The registration of citizens and their property in ancient Rome, usu. for taxation purposes. M17. **3** An official enumeration of the population of a country etc., or of a class of things, usu. with statistics relating to them. M18 **B** *v.t.* Conduct a census of; count, enumerate. L19.

The 'E17' in this definition suggests that the use of the word 'census' in English dates only from the early seventeenth century. However, the use of the Latin term *cense* dates from the days of the Roman Empire. Through the Bible, Britons were aware of the Roman census, although not necessarily of its full significance. Christians marking the birth of Jesus each Christmas were familiar with the words from the Gospel of St Luke (2, 1–3):

> And it came to pass in those days, that there went out a decree from Caesar Augustus, that all the world should be taxed. (And this taxing was first made when Cyrenius was governor of Syria.) And all went to be taxed, every one into his own city.

This census of circa AD 0^1 was thus the alleged reason that Jesus' mother Mary and her husband, Joseph, were travelling from Nazareth to Bethlehem, where the baby was believed to be born. At the time, citizens of the Roman Empire had to register for the census in their place of family origin. As Joseph was descended from the line of David, he had to register in Bethlehem, the town of David in Judea. Historians have questioned this, arguing that no such movement of people was required. Nevertheless, the Roman census was taken quinquennially between 550 BC and AD 14. Before the mid-fourth century BC, the statistics are regarded as unreliable.

The earliest recorded census was of Mesopotamia in 3800 BC under the command of the king of Babylonia. The purpose of all the early censuses was to establish resources of both finance and human beings. The Babylonians recorded the number of pigs, among other produce in their lands, while the Romans monitored numbers of men available for taxation purposes, as well as for their extensive armies.

In the seventh century AD, a census was taken of the kingdoms of the *Dal Riata*, the Gaelic lands that now form part of Scotland and Northern Ireland. This census is contained with royal genealogies in the *Senchus Fer n-Alban* (*History of the Men of Scotland*), and reveals how the population was divided within fiscal and military groups.

Like the rulers of Babylon and of Rome, after William the Conqueror had settled in England, he wanted to establish the numbers of men and resources available to him. This resulted in a form of census known as the *Domesday Book*, the original of which is held at The National Archives. The assessment, begun in 1085, recorded 13,418 settlements of the counties south of the rivers Ribble and Tees. More than twenty royal commissioners acted as census enumerators in seven circuits (regions).

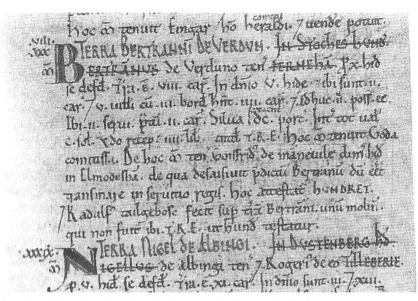

Page from Domesday Book showing the entry for Bertram de Verdun.

It concentrated on the king's property and land, providing details of the nature of the land, any buildings and the resources of the land (e.g. fish, animals, plants). A jury of local people gave the names of the landholders (tenants-in-chief), tenants and under-tenants to the royal commissioners. The social position of the tenants as villagers, smallholders, free men or slaves was also identified. Urban entries include records of traders.

Not everyone was included. Only heads of households were recorded and notable absences from the book are nuns, monks and people living in castles, as well as the inhabitants of London, Winchester, Bristol, the borough of Tamworth and the lands that became Westmoreland, Cumberland, Northumberland and Durham. The book remained incomplete: work on the survey was abandoned in 1087, during the reign of William Rufus.

In 1676, the Bishop of London, Henry Compton, initiated an ecclesiastical survey of individual parishes. The Compton census, as this is commonly known, aimed to discover an estimate of the numbers of Anglicans (Conformists), Catholic recusants (Papists), and Protestant Dissenters (Nonconformists) in England and Wales. As may be expected from this early census, results were inconsistent. The incumbent was asked:

1stly What number of persons are there by common Account & estimation inhabiting within each parish subject to your jurisdiction?

2dly What number of Popish Recusants or persons suspected for such Recusancy are there resident amongst the Inhabitants aforesaid?

3dly What number of other Dissenters are there in each parish of what Sect soever which either obstinately refuse or wholly absent themselves from the Communion of the Church of England at such times as by law they are required.

The total number of people in the parish was intended to include only those of 16 years and over, but this instruction was often misinterpreted. There is evidence of omissions from the census, such as the cottagers of the parish of Llandaff.[2] Besides this, some Protestant Dissenters attended church as well as chapel, and were thus recorded twice.

The census was administered by the deaconries and arch-deaconries. As such, where original returns survive, they may be found in individual archdeaconry records. Most exist only in the form of an eighteenth-century manuscript held at the William Salt Library in Stafford. Anne Whiteman has edited the returns and they are now available to read in book form: Anne Whiteman (ed.) (with Mary Clapinson), *The Compton Census of 1676: A Critical Edition* (British Academy: Records of Social and Economic History, N.S. 10, 1986).

How and Why Were the Nineteenth-Century Census Records Created?

From the mid-eighteenth century, the census in Western Europe and America became more of an official enumeration of the population of a country, rather than merely an exercise in resource-counting. This was influenced, in part, by the writings of the French philosopher Jean Bodin (1529/30–96). In his *Six Books of the Commonwealth* (1576), Bodin acknowledged the usefulness of censuses for establishing military availability, colonial personnel and a domestic labour force. He also praised their ability to identify how members of the population were occupied and what property they owned, such as in the 1471 census of Provence. Bodin respected the Roman *censor*'s role as not merely an enumerator but as the officer responsible for public morality. The census, through the medium of its censor, therefore, was responsible for maintaining the high standards of the Roman Empire and its tight control on tax abuse.

Bodin's ideas influenced attitudes to the census during the period of the Enlightenment in the late seventeenth and eighteenth centuries. The Enlightenment's focus on knowledge and understanding of everything inspired politicians across Europe to introduce censuses of their populations. From Sweden in 1749, to Norway and Denmark in 1769, to German states in 1776, and Austria and Spain in 1787, the rulers of Western Europe sought to fully know their citizens through the medium of the census. From this knowledge, governments could exert greater control of their populations, not just for military or economic purposes, but for social and moral ends, too. The first country to introduce a regular census was the United States in 1790. Britain soon followed, initiating her first census eleven years later in 1801.[3]

Before 1801, rulers of specific parts of Britain had conducted their own censuses, usually when planning their local militia. In a few cases, names can be found in what survives of these census records. Some local overseers created nominal lists to assist with the administration, but most only named the head of the household.

In 1753, Thomas Potter (1718–59), a Member of Parliament, had tried to introduce an annual census to take place from 1754, but his bill failed to pass in the House of Commons. This failure was largely due to the lobbying of landed gentry, who feared a census would lead to higher taxes on property owners. However, the revolutions in America (1777) and France (1789) stirred new fears among Britain's elite of potential uprising by their own servants and labourers. Other fears were generated by contemporary wars. As America and France had taken censuses of their populations and thus had greater knowledge of their people, British politicians feared this might give the enemy an advantage. Other socio-political thinkers had a more philanthropic motive for wanting a census. They wanted to know more about the increasing urban poor: where and how they lived, how many there were, where they came from and the nature of their work. The resulting knowledge was intended to be used to improve the lives of the poor.[4]

In the meantime, Potter's efforts had influenced others, including members of the Royal Society and fellow MPs. A statistician, John Rickman (1771–1840), who later served as a clerk in the House of Commons, wrote a memorandum in 1796 entitled 'Thoughts on the Utility and Facility of a General Enumeration of the People of the British Empire.' This was brought to the attention of MP and Royal Society Fellow Charles Abbot (1757–1829, later 1st Baron Colchester), by George Rose, MP (who later introduced Rose's Act of 1812). With Abbot's support, Rickman's ideas had a great effect on Parliament and led a few years later to the 'Act for taking Account of the Population of Great Britain, and of the Increase in Diminution thereof' of 1800.

Commonly referred to as the Census (Population) Act of 1800, this established a regular national census, which would be taken every ten years from 1801. The resulting census data from 1801, 1811, 1821 and 1831 is stored at The National Archives (TNA) in Kew. The reports are entitled 'Abstracts of the Answers and Returns made pursuant to an Act for taking account of the Population of Great Britain, and of the increase or diminution thereof.'

The new census was overseen by John Rickman, whom Abbot appointed as his private secretary in 1800. Rickman would be rewarded for his work when he was appointed a Fellow of the Royal Society in 1815. He was recognized not just in Britain, but also in Europe, where he received a diploma as honorary membership of the Société Française de Statistique Universelle in 1833.

In his memorandum, Rickman wrote: 'It will be intuitively granted that an intimate knowledge of a country can be the only foundation of the legislation of that country, and also of its political relation to other nations.'[5] The population census gave the government information on societal patterns, which would be useful for military recruitment during the contemporary war with France. The 1801 census is, however, of limited use to family historians as it consists of statistics of households but contains few names.

The Historical Use of Censuses

On Tuesday, 10 March 1801 in England, Scotland and Wales, the first national census of Britain was taken. This census did not cover the Channel Islands, the Isle of Man or Ireland. The overseers of the poor for each parish (or township, tithing or quarter) were asked to collect certain information on their respective parishes. If they knew the details, they were not required to ask their parishioners. With this information, they filled in the schedule returns which were then sent to the Secretary of State for the Home Office.[6]

- HOUSES
  Inhabited
  By how many Families occupied
  Un-inhabited
- PERSONS
  Males
  Females
- OCCUPATIONS
  Persons chiefly employed in Agriculture
  Persons chiefly employed in Trade, Manufactures, or Handicraft
- TOTAL OF PERSONS
  All other Persons not comprised in the Two Preceding Classes.

This census did not ask for ages, which limited its usefulness in providing statistics of potential military recruits. It also neglected men serving in the armed forces and militia, as well as merchant seamen.

In 1811, questions were similar, but not identical, to those of 1801. The occupation questions asked for the number of families engaged in trade, agriculture and so on. One purpose of this was to monitor dwindling numbers of those engaged in family-based labour. Results would show how the population was moving away from family-based jobs into industrial roles in the ever-expanding towns and cities. This census, which was taken on Monday, 27 May, also differentiated the number of uninhabited houses between those that were abandoned and those that were being built. Although the questions were answered by the overseers of English and Welsh parishes, in Scotland they were answered by local schoolmasters.

Questions

1st. How many Inhabited Houses are there in your Parish, Township, or Place; and by how many Families are they occupied?

2d. How many Houses are now building, and therefore not yet inhabited?

3d. How many other Houses are uninhabited?

4th. What Number of Families in your Parish, Township, or Place, are chiefly employed in and maintained by Agriculture; how many Families are chiefly employed in and maintained by Trade, Manufactures, or Handicraft; and how many Families are not comprised in either of the two preceding Classes?

5th. How many Persons (including Children of whatever Age) are there actually found within the Limits of your Parish, Township, or Place, *at the Time of taking this Account*, distinguishing Males and Females, and *exclusive* of Men actually serving in His Majesty's Regular Forces, in the Old Militia, or in any *Embodied* Local Militia, and *exclusive* of Seamen either in His Majesty's Service or belonging to Registered Vessels?

6th. Referring to the number of Persons in 1801, To what Cause do you attribute any remarkable Difference in the number at present?

7th. Are there any other Matters, which you may think it necessary to remark, in Explanation of your Answers to any of the preceding Questions?

Results of the censuses could, from this point on, be found in local newspapers. Care should be taken with this, however, as some of these published results were unofficial and thus unreliable. These can be accessed at the relevant local archives or (depending on title) online at the British Newspaper Archive:

The first attempt to take an Official Census in this country was made in 1813, pursuant to an Act passed in 1812. Under this statute the supervision of the enumeration was entrusted to the Grand Juries of the several counties. This arrangement worked badly, the Grand Juries, from their constitution, not being capable of efficiently superintending the work, and having at their disposal no adequate machinery for its accomplishment...[A]fter two years spent in a fruitless endeavour...the attempt was abandoned.

The failure of this inquiry directed public attention to the necessity of providing more effective machinery, and an Act was passed in 1815 vesting the superintendence of the next census in the Magistrates at Quarter Sessions and the Assistant Barristers; and accordingly the Census of 1821 was taken under their supervision. Though there was no staff officially under the control of the magistrates, yet the nomination of the enumerators was placed in their hands, and much care appears to have been taken to secure the services of men who were competent to perform the duty. At first many difficulties appeared. In some districts open hostility manifested itself, while in others the undefined state of the boundaries caused many obstacles to the compilation of a satisfactory statistical return. These, however, having been surmounted, the results of the first authoritative and complete Irish Census were presented to the public in 1823.

A second enumeration of the people was taken in 1831. The inquiry, however, was not commenced simultaneously in all parts of the country, and it extended over a considerable period. The Enumerators, moreover, were under the impression that they would be paid in proportion to the numbers they enumerated, a system of payment which, it appears, was in many cases actually adopted. For these and other reasons, the results of this Census have not been regarded as satisfactory.

The Census of 1841 opened a new era in Irish Statistics. It was then for the first time that the Ordnance Survey maps were available, and a regularly organized police force – the Constabulary – at hand, from which a corps of Enumerators could be selected. The Commissioners of 1841 were also the first to employ Forms of Family Return, to be filled by the Head of the Family instead of having the particulars entered by the Enumerator from *viva voce* inquiry. Their report deals with the population viewed in most of its social aspects, and it has rightly been regarded as a model of succinctness.

The Census of 1851 was taken under the superintendence of the Registrar-General of Marriages, Mr. William Donnelly, assisted by Dr. (afterwards Sir) William Wilde. The chief features of that enumeration were the School Census and the Report on the Status of Disease, which, in addition to treating of the number of people suffering from sickness, dealt with the deaf and dumb, the blind, the lunatic and idiotic, and the lame and decrepit. An interesting Table of Cosmical Phenomena, Epizootics, Famines and Pestilences in Ireland, from the earliest records published, was also compiled by the Assistant Commissioner, aided by the eminent Irish scholars, Dr. O'Donovan and Mr. Eugene O'Curry, MRIA. The Agricultural Statistics (first commenced in 1847) for 1851 and 1852 were collected by the Commissioners, who also published detailed statistics of emigration.

The first national census of Ireland was taken between 1813 and 1815.[7] This was legislated by the Census (Ireland) Act of 1812 (52 Geo. III c.133), which appears to have been based on the British census of 1811. The Irish census was conducted by mainly Protestant parish officers and barony constables. This led to conflict with the many Catholic householders, some of whom refused to co-operate. Consequently, the census produced few results, but an abstract was published in 1822 and can be viewed on the Online Historical Populations Report (HISTPOP).[8]

The 1821 census was taken on Monday, 28 May. Ireland was for the first time included in the census-taking. However, it was enumerated and reported separately from those of the English, Welsh and Scottish censuses. The Isle of Man and the Channel Islands were also enumerated for the first time this year. The questions on this occasion divided the population by age groups (left to the discretion of overseers). One of the purposes of this was to discover rates of life expectancy, the details of which would be used by insurance companies. Disappointingly for the said companies, the results of this census were never fully completed.

Questions

1st. How many Inhabited Houses are there in your Parish, Township, or Place; and by how many Families are they occupied?

2d. How many Houses are now building, and therefore not yet inhabited?

3d. How many other Houses are Inhabited?

4th. What Number of Families in your Parish, Township, or Place, are chiefly employed in and maintained by Agriculture, or by Trade, manufacture, or Handicraft; and how many Families are not comprised in either of the Two preceding Classes?

5th. How many Persons (including Children of whatever Age) are there actually found within the Limits of your Parish, Township, or place, at the Time of taking this Account, distinguishing Males and Females, and exclusive of Men actually serving in His Majesty's Regular Forces, in the Old Militia, or in any embodied Local Militia, and exclusive of Seamen either in His Majesty's Service, or belonging to Registered Vessels?

6th. Referring to the Number of Persons in one thousand eight hundred and eleven, To what Cause do you attribute any remarkable Difference in the Number at present?

7th. If you are of Opinion that in making the preceding Enquiries (or at any Time before returning this Schedule,) the Ages of the several Individuals can be obtained in a Manner satisfactory to yourself, and not inconvenient to the Parties, be pleased to state (or cause to be stated) the Number of those who are under 5 Years of Age, of those between 5 and 10 Years of Age, between 10 and 15, between 15 and 20, between 20 and 30, between 30 and 40, between 40 and 50, between 50 and 60, between 60 and 70, between 70 and 80, between 80 and 90, between 90 and 100, and upwards of 100, distinguishing Males from Females – And are there any other Matters which you may think it necessary to remark in Explanation of your Answer to this or any of the preceding Questions – And in what Manner and to what Place of Residence and Post Office Town are Letters intended for you usually directed?

The census of Monday, 30 May 1831 was to be the last census overseen by John Rickman. Although similar in design to the previous censuses, the 1831 census would differ by extending the age columns by asking males whether they were above or below the age of 20. This information would be used for assessing the military potential of the population. However, there was no question that would help the politicians to learn about the ages or mortality levels of women and children. In order to further assess industrial growth, the census asked about occupational details for males aged over 20. Again, the large section of the working population that consisted of women and children was completely ignored.

Questions

1st. How many Inhabited Houses are there in your Parish, Township, or Place; and by how many Families are they occupied?

2d. How many Houses are now building, and therefore not yet inhabited?

3d. How many other Houses are uninhabited?

4th. What Number of Families in your Parish, Township, or Place, are chiefly employed in and maintained by Agriculture; or by Trade, Manufacture, or Handicraft; and how many Families are not comprised in either of the Two preceding Classes?

5th. How many Persons (including Children of whatever Age) are there actually found within the Limits of your Parish, Township, or place, at the Time of taking this Account, distinguishing Males and Females, and exclusive of Men actually serving in His Majesty's Regular Forces, in the Old Militia, or in any embodied Local Militia, and exclusive of Seamen either in His Majesty's Service, or belonging to Registered Vessels?

6th. How many of the Males enumerated in answer to the 5th Question are upwards of Twenty Years old?

7th. How many Males upwards of Twenty Years old are employed in Agriculture, including Graziers, Cowkeepers, Shepherds, and other Farm Servants, Gardeners (not taxed or taxable as Male Servants), and Nurserymen?

8th. How many Males upwards of Twenty Years old are employed in Manufacture or in making Manufacturing Machinery; *but not including Labourers in Warehouses, Porters, Messengers, &c.; who are to be included in a subsequent Class*?

9th. How many Males upwards of Twenty Years old are employed in Retail trade or in Handicraft; as Masters, Shopmen, Journeymen, Apprentices, or in any Capacity requiring Skill in the Business; *but not including Labourers, Porters, Messengers, &c. who are to be included in a subsequent Class*?

10th. How many males upwards of Twenty Years old are *Wholesale Merchants, Bankers, Capitalists, Professional Persons, Artists, Architects, teachers, Clerks, Surveyors, and other Educated Men? And in answering this Question, you will include generally Persons maintaining themselves otherwise than by Manufacture, Trade, or bodily Labour.

[*A Retailer sells to the Consumer the Article sold.]

11th. How many males upwards of Twenty Years old are Miners, Fishermen, Boatmen, Excavators of Canals, Roadmakers, Toll Collectors, or Labourers employed by Persons of the Three preceding Classes, [Questions 8th, 9th, 10th,] or otherwise employed in any Kind of bodily Labour, excepting *in Agriculture*? Labourer in Agriculture having been already entered in the proper Place.

12th. How many other Males upwards of Twenty Years old (not being taxable Servants under the next Question) have not been included in any of the foregoing Classes? Including, therefore, in answer to this Question, retired Tradesmen, Superannuated Labourers, and Males diseased or disabled in Body or Mind.

13th. How many Household Servants, including all Female Servants, and such Male Servants (of whatever Age) as are taxed or taxable as such; also Waiters and Attendants at Inns; distinguishing the Males upwards of Twenty Years of Age from the Males under Twenty Years of Age?

14th. If you have entered any Males in answer to the 8th Question, be please to specify Manufacture or Manufactures in which they are employed; and what Proportion of the Number of those entered in answer to Question 11th are employed in any Quarry, Mines, Coal Pits, Fishery, or public Work now in progress?

15th. Referring to the number of Persons in the year 1821, to what cause do you attribute any remarkable difference in the number at present?

16th. Are there any other matters which you may think it necessary to remark in explanation of your answers to any of the preceding Questions?

By the time of the 1841 census, John Rickman had died and a new monarch was on the throne. During the 1820s and 1830s, criticisms had been raised that Britain's statistical system was too simplistic. The political economist J.R. McCulloch accused it of being 'discreditable to the nation'. On 15 March 1834, the Statistical Society of London[9] was formed by a group that included its first president, the statesman Henry Petty-Fitzmaurice, 3rd Marquess of Landsdowne, the mathematician, Charles Babbage, and the population theorist, Reverend Thomas Malthus. Scotland quickly followed, with the Statistical Society of Glasgow (1836) and, later, the Edinburgh Medico-Statistical Association (1852).

Philosophers and statisticians were now agreed that a different approach was required, and that the system of the census needed to be altered radically. In 1840, a committee of men from the London Statistical Society (LSS) made suggestions to be implemented in the census of the following year. Among its more successful suggestions was that of naming individuals and noting their details on household schedules, using enumerator transcripts to collate each household's details, and of tabulating all the data in one place.

From 1841 onwards, statisticians and politicians were able to use the census data for further purposes, notably to trace mortality and morbidity over time. This would later influence developments in town planning, public sanitation and housing. Particularly active in the use of census data for public health were the medical statistician Dr William Farr, the founder of epidemiology John Snow and the nursing pioneer Florence Nightingale. The population statistics were combined with date of birth, marriage and death records, schools and poor law boards to plan and influence government policy and social reform. Census reports were used well into the twentieth century to provide evidence to support changes to housing policy, such as with the *New Survey of London Life and Labour* in 1930.

Current Uses of Historical Censuses

In the twenty-first century, historical censuses are accessed a great deal. Academics, statisticians, social theorists, economists, demographers, policy reformers and others continue to use censuses in much the way that they were intended by John Rickman, such as monitoring population levels. Historians can also use the census material in this way, but newer ways of looking at and learning from the census have emerged from the twentieth century. These include local, socio-economic and house history, as well as genealogy. Recent assessments of the censuses have considered changes in religious adherence, mortality rates and looked at changes in immigration and emigration over extended periods of time.

Since the 1960s, family historians have been inspired to use these censuses for their research. This is in many ways due to the work of D.J. (Don) Steel (1935–2008) and his Berkshire listings in 'Earlier Censuses – Parish Censuses' in *The National Index of Parish Registers*, vol. 1, *Sources of Births, Marriages and Deaths before 1837*, part I, pp.333–6 (Society of Genealogists, 1968). Steel was active at the time in the area of one-name studies. From there, the work of Colin Chapman, Mervyn Medlycott and Jeremy Gibson has brought awareness of the use of censuses to a wider genealogy audience.

In the 1970s and 1980s, genealogists travelled to the Land Registry in Portugal Street, London to examine the censuses of 1841–71 on microfilm. From here, the microfilms were moved to the Public Record Office (PRO) in London's Chancery Lane. In 1997, copies of these microfilms were made available to family historians who used the newly opened Family Records Centre in Clerkenwell. That closed in 2008, after census usage had been transferred, for the most part, to online resources. Today, family historians can access censuses using a variety of online databases. This has enabled new ways of searching for, and examining, census material.

Microfilm or microfiche copies of the 1841–1901 census returns are available at most local record offices and Church of Jesus Christ of Latter-Day Saints' (LDS) family history centres. Many libraries in the UK offer free access on site, or via a library card, to library editions of subscription sites, such as Ancestry and / or Findmypast.

There are a number of commercial and free census data providers online:

Ancestry
Ancestry.com

Coverage: Indexes and images of census records from England, Wales, the Channel Islands and the Isle of Man, covering 1841–1911. Scottish census indexes and transcriptions for 1841–1901 inclusive. Free index for the 1881 census of England, Wales and the Islands in the British Seas, and for the UK census free sample. 1939 England and Wales Register.

Features: General and flexible search range. Can also search on the specific census.

Estimate ages to within 1, 2, 5 or 10 years. Search option of forename only. Wildcard search using '*' after first or before last character and beside three non-wildcard letters.

Census details and image can be saved to the online Ancestry family tree. The quality of the transcriptions varies, with 1881 being reported by users as the most accurate. Criticism of the Scottish transcriptions; praise for the source referencing of Scottish censuses.

Many genealogists say Ancestry is very easy to search from either the home page of the website, or the specific census or census year pages. Genealogists have praised its useful and accurate list of results, as well as its inclusion of birthplace in the search results. On a practical level, users like the zoom option, magnifier print and saving options.

However, critics complain of a poor layout and that too many unrelated results are returned; there are a high number of transcription errors, and it can be hard to find an ancestor in the general search if any transcription errors have occurred. Browsing by place is problematic, and changes in place names over time can be difficult to search. Spelling is not corrected but alternatives are provided. Scottish transcriptions are limited, with no recording of language spoken or infirmities, but are respected for their accuracy.

TheGenealogist
TheGenealogist.co.uk

Coverage: Census transcriptions and images for 1841–1911. Set up as S&N Genealogy. The company also produces software and data products.

Features: TheGenealogist master search allows for general and flexible searching by name of person, family or address (house & street). Includes an option of searching by keyword, such as an occupation, name or place. Gives the street address in the results. Other options (basic and advanced) to search individual censuses by year and county. Crew lists of 1861, 1871 and 1901. Also offers 1821 and 1831 censuses for London (Marylebone), and a 1921 census substitute (taken from various sources). Many genealogists like the simple layout, but are confused by the subscription options. TheGenealogist has volunteer census indexes; subscription-holders can access these without using any of their search credits.

Some images are clearer than on other sites.

Findmypast
Findmypast.com

Coverage: Original images and (the company claims) 'the most full and accurate transcriptions online' for England, Wales, the Isle of Man and the Channel Islands 1841–1911 censuses. Indexes and transcriptions for Scottish censuses 1841–1901. Free indexes and basic transcriptions. Free fuller transcription for 1881. Subscriptions for image viewing.

Features: Offers a search of censuses via a general database option, or by specific census year. Offers a person search, an address search and a census reference search.

Advanced searches are also available. Genealogists have praised the simple layout of the search and results pages, especially the use of full addresses. They find the search options easy to use. They also highlight the ability to search name variables, locating members of the armed forces who are serving overseas, and to search on more than one named person in a house at once. There is praise for the address and occupation searches as well as the accuracy of the transcriptions, particularly of those in Scotland. Errors in transcriptions are fixed when reported.

Critics argue that the results are haphazard and that the referencing for Scottish censuses is poor. Transcriptions are incomplete.

Genes Reunited
www.genesreunited.co.uk

Coverage: This covers indexes, transcriptions and images for 1841–1911. Also includes Scottish census transcriptions for 1841–1901, Corfe Castle and District 1790 Census, and Nether Hallam, Sheffield 1831 Census.

Features: Offers subscription and pay-per-view searches. Details can be saved to the online family tree.

FamilySearch
www.familysearch.org

Coverage: Incomplete indexes and basic transcriptions are available for the English and Welsh censuses of 1841–1911, and the Scottish 1841–91 censuses. Links to images provided (via subscription) by **Findmypast. com**.

Features: Free. Genealogists often use this site first to find a person or family, and then use that to consult the image on a commercial site. Searching by date of birth on this site can be successful. The accuracy of the transcriptions, particularly of 1881, is praised. There has been criticism of the new layout, which some find confusing.

FreeCEN
www.freecen.org.uk

Coverage: Provides indexes and transcriptions to English, Scottish and Welsh censuses for 1841–91.

Features: Free. Genealogists praise the quality of the transcriptions. Good coverage of Scottish censuses. Coverage is not comprehensive.

ScotlandsPeople
www.scotlandspeople.gov.uk

Coverage: The only website to give full access to the images of the Scottish 1841–1911 censuses. Provides search indexes and transcriptions of 1841–1911 censuses. Includes an 1881 LDS census search and transcription for free.

Features: Search censuses by individual year. Wildcards can be used in the address search. When a census image is viewed, the header page (the enumerator's description) can be viewed at no extra cost. Street indexes are available on the site. Critics complain of the paucity of search fields.

Scottish Indexes
https://www.scottishindexes.com/recordsets.aspx

Coverage: Free searches of the indexes to the 1841, 1851 and 1861 Scottish censuses, as well as pre-1841 censuses and population lists. The results of the searches link to free transcriptions.

Features: Offers searches by name, occupation, address/place, birth year and birthplace. Coverage for the 1841 census is limited to Berwickshire, Peeblesshire, Roxburghshire and Selkirkshire, with parts of Dumfriesshire, East Lothian and Midlothian. Coverage for 1851 is limited to Berwickshire, Dumfriesshire, Peeblesshire, Roxburghshire and Selkirkshire, as well as parts of East Lothian, Kirkcudbrightshire, Lanarkshire, Midlothian and Wigtownshire. The 1861 census covers Berwickshire, Peeblesshire, Roxburghshire and Selkirkshire, along with parts of Dumfriesshire, East Lothian and Midlothian.

Census of Ireland 1901/1911 and Census fragments and substitutes, 1821–51
www.census.nationalarchives.ie

Coverage: Provides indexes, transcriptions and images of the household returns and ancillary records for the Irish censuses of 1901 and 1911.

The 1901 and 1911 censuses are the only complete surviving census records for the pre-Independence period. Fragments survive for 1821–1851 for some counties, as follows:

Antrim, 1851; Belfast city (one ward only), 1851; Cavan, 1821 and 1841; Cork, 1841; Dublin city (index to heads of household only), 1851; Fermanagh, 1821, 1841 and 1851; Galway, 1813 (numerical returns for Longford barony) and 1821; King's County (Offaly), 1821; Londonderry (Derry), 1831–34; Meath, 1821; Waterford, 1841.

Features: Free. The official Irish census website from The National Archives of Ireland. Search on all information categories: year, surname, forename, county, barony (except 1821), parish and townland/street. The 1841 and 1851 censuses usefully list members of the household not at home on census night, and also family members who died since 1831/1841.

Emerald Ancestors
http://www.emeraldancestors.com/index.asp

Coverage: Northern Irish census records on a commercial website.

Features: The census records feature among the Ulster ancestry database. They include 1901 Fermanagh census, Northern Ireland census extracts 1841–51 and a nineteenth-century census collection.

RootsUK
www.rootsuk.com
Coverage: Complete census images with transcripts. Data provided by TheGenealogist.
Features: Similar options to TheGenealogist.

UK Indexer
www.UKindexer.co.uk
Coverage: Volunteers who transcribe parish or other records receive free vouchers and subscriptions to TheGenealogist.
Features: Free access to some records for volunteer transcribers.

UK Census Online
www.ukcensusonline.com
Coverage: Complete set of census records from England and Wales for 1841–1911, including transcripts and images of original documents.
Features: Searching the census is free but to view the full details and images a subscription must be bought. Saves money by paying only for censuses rather than the extra features of other databases.

A full set of historical census reports is held by the British Library. These reports provide aggregate statistical information for each census question. The Library's maps department holds detailed historical census maps which clarify the population differences in different parts of Britain and Ireland. The reports for 1921–91 are held on the open shelves in the Social Sciences Reading Room. Reports and other census material are also held at academic libraries. This can be identified via the COPAC internet search engine (**http://copac.ac.uk/search**). Regional census reports should be found at local archives. The Vision of Britain website, in association with the Historical Geographic Information System (GIS) Project, based at the University of Portsmouth, contains census reports from 1801 to 1961 with direct access to the main tables.

All complete published census reports for England, Wales, Scotland and Ireland, 1801–1937 (bar the 1926 census of the Irish Free State) can be found at the Online Historical Populations Report (HISTPOP), **www.histpop.org**. These reports are not used generally for family history purposes, but can be useful for providing social and economic context. They are helpful for local historians and can be searched by place. In the 'Legislation' section of the website database are the full texts of all the Acts of Parliament relating to the census, dating back to 1801.

Vision of Britain website.

There are problems with interpreting the returns, and family historians should question the information given by their families to the enumerators; for example, regarding the nature of employment. In the Victorian period, part-time, seasonal and casual employment were common. The employment or unemployment of an ancestor on a census does not necessarily tell us what he or she was doing for the previous or next ten years, or even the next week. Working-class men may have had multiple occupations at once, but this is rarely recorded on the census. Feminist historians have long argued that women's employment status has been misrepresented on the census, with thousands of women's jobs simply ignored by the enumerator, particularly those who worked from home or with their husband.

The terms used can also be problematic. Although 'labourer' and 'scholar' were defined for the enumerators (see Glossary), these and other terms were often interpreted differently by individual householders and even some enumerators.

Why Some People Are Not Found on Censuses

There can be a number of reasons why individuals cannot be found on censuses as expected. These include names being wrongly transcribed, incorrect spellings or being difficult to read. Sometimes people may simply not have been recorded on the census. In other cases, pieces of the censuses have been destroyed, damaged or are otherwise missing.

Where names have been wrongly transcribed, it is worth checking different indexes or websites produced by alternative transcribers.

Besides the wrong appearance of a name, there is the possibility that an individual is enumerated under a different name from what was expected. This may be a formal name, nickname, middle name, shortened version of the name, or women recorded under their maiden name. Others may have the surname of their stepfather, mother's common-law husband, a lodger or others above them in the household schedule (e.g. servants given the surname of their masters). Men may be found with the surname of a woman with whom they were cohabiting. Recent immigrants or others with a surname of foreign origin may have changed their name from the foreign spelling (e.g. Goodman instead of Gottman), or otherwise may be using an alias.

In the early years particularly, ancestors may not be found as they were travellers, members of the armed forces, merchant seamen, or had gone abroad. Some individuals absented themselves from the census deliberately: they may have worried about being recorded for fear of tax, official knowledge of their whereabouts or to hide away from legal authorities or estranged spouses. Others, for example suffragettes in 1911, boycotted the census as a political protest.

Parts of each census are either missing from The National Archives' collection or no longer exist. In some cases, entries have faded or been destroyed. Specific details will be explored in the chapters on each census, but the census with the most missing sections is that of 1861. Some of these were destroyed by poor storage, while others were lost en route to the Registrar General in London.

A few cases exist of individuals being arrested and even prosecuted for absenting themselves from the census.[10]

Records of People in Institutions and the Homeless

Identifying the correct person in the censuses of institutions, such as prisons, workhouses, hospitals or lunatic asylums, can be difficult. Often minimal details are included, such as inmates being recorded with initials only. The use of general geographic areas in the birthplace column (from 1851) – such as 'London' or 'Scotland' without mention of a parish or even the wrong parish completely – is common. This also occurs with records of the armed forces and boarding schools.

Homeless people who slept on the streets are not usually enumerated. Those who were sheltered in an institution, even if only for census night, however, should be recorded. Besides workhouses, there were asylums dedicated to those with no home. In Hackney, on the 1861 census these included the Refuge for the Destitute, Dalston. Located in St Giles Bloomsbury was the Refuge for Homeless and Destitute Girls. Homeless children may be found in orphanages, workhouses or industrial homes. Other homeless people who avoided asylums may be found enumerated with relatives or as lodgers.

Those whose work or lifestyle may have excluded them from one or more censuses are examined further in the chapters on the respective censuses from 1841 onwards.

Chapter 2

EARLY CENSUSES

Surviving Pre-1841 Censuses

Before 1801, a number of private censuses were taken by individual politicians, bishops and landowners. These were not national censuses, but do include names. In some cases, only the heads of household or males of a certain age are named. Nevertheless, family historians can find the records useful for researching a specific area or for understanding parts of British society in a given year. One of the earliest known of these surveys was taken in Ealing in 1599. The original records are held at The National Archives, ref. E 163/24/35, but the names and ages of those surveyed have been published in K.J. Allison's 'An Elizabethan Village Census', *Bulletin of the Institute of Historical Research* 36 (1963), pp.91–103 and other publications.

Of the various types of religious or ecclesiastical censuses taken, many were administered by church wardens. Although most of these records were created by Anglican churches, they often include names of Nonconformists who lived in the parish. Some even contain details of key events, family relationships, occupations and sketched maps of the area surveyed. Most of the original records are held in local archives, but some have been transcribed and published. Copies may be found at larger libraries and at the Society of Genealogists.

In the 1970s, historians began referring to these records as 'local censuses'. It is not known how many local censuses survive or how complete they are. In their attempt to find out, Jeremy Gibson and Mervyn Medlycott discovered more than 750 parish listings dating from 1801. In their guide to the subject, *Local Census Listings 1522–1930* (1994), they note which of these records include names of parish inhabitants. In England and Wales, names were not recorded on the national censuses of 1801, 1811, 1821 and 1831 that were used for government purposes.

However, they may be found on these local lists, which were often retained for reasons of local poor law administration. The names were not sent to London with the census statistics books, but instead were kept locally.

The original national census records of 1801–31 were destroyed in 1904. All that survives are the statistics that were reported in the Parliamentary Papers, which can be found on HISTPOP, and the clergymen's returns of numbers of baptisms, marriages and burials by parish (1821–30), which is held at The National Archives, ref. HO 71.

In Ireland, where national censuses were first taken in 1821, the enumerators did ask for full details from households. Although most parts of the Irish censuses were destroyed, a few do survive; of these, most contain names. More details are found below.

Pender's Census, 1659

Religious and civil censuses were also taken in Ireland before 1801. In 1659, Sir William Petty was tasked to list the names of tituladoes (those with title to land), the number of English and Irish in each townland, and the principal Irish names in each barony. The census did not cover the counties of Cavan, Galway, Mayo, Tyrone and Wicklow. The census was edited by Seamus Pender and first published in 1939.[1] It is often referred to as 'Pender's Census'.

Bishop Bowers' Survey, 1724

Similar to Bishop Compton's census were the diocesan surveys of the parishes of Sussex, which took place in 1686 and 1724. Bishop Bowers' Survey of 1724 asked thirteen questions relating to the parish church, its incumbent, the number of families in the parish and the numbers of Nonconformists. The Bishop Bowers' Visitation Book Ep/I/26/3 is held at West Sussex Record Office.

Religious Census of Ireland, 1766

In 1766, a religious census of Ireland was taken. Like the later national censuses of 1821–71, the transcripts of this census were stored in the Public Records Office of Ireland in the Four Courts, Dublin. This building, and much of its content, was destroyed by fire in 1922. Only a few censuses survived. Among these were fragments of the 1766 religious census, which had been copied out by Tennison Groves. These are held at the National Library. Some have been microfilmed by the LDS (film references 100173 and 100220). The census fragments contain 11,000 names of heads of households, together with their religion

(Protestant, Catholic or Dissenter) and name of parish or townland. The heads of households include single women and widows. The LDS film transcriptions have been digitized for Ancestry.

National and Local Censuses 1801–31

From the earliest 1801 national censuses for England, Wales and Scotland, surviving records include the abstracts. These are held in the Parliamentary Archives and can be seen online in academic and larger libraries via the House of Commons Parliamentary Paper database. The completed schedules that were sent to the Secretary of State for the Home Office have not survived.

The abstracts of 1801 include details from parish registers, such as numbers of marriages for 1754–1800, and baptisms/burials at intervals.[2] As 1801 was the first national census in Britain, some parish officials failed to complete their instructions. Consequently, some did not return their schedules and their parishes are not represented in the records.

The 1801 *Abstract, presented to the House of Commons, of the answers and returns made to the Population Act of 41st Geo. III. &c.* provides a list of each county and records whether parish detail is missing or 'wanting'. Parishes with wanting returns included 'the Town of Newbury', the 'entire Hundred of Chilford', 'Five Cinque Ports and Members of the same', 'Grantham and Soke ... and Stamford Borough', 'a few Inns of Court', 'More than Half of the County' of Monmouth, 'Worplesdon, near Guildford', 'The Wapentake of Osgoldness' and 'the Hamlet of Clynamon'. Other problems noted in the abstract were that in Middlesex (by this date Middlesex included a major section of the London parishes north of the Thames) figures for the number of families would be distorted as many parishes 'returned each Lodger as a separate Family'. At this time the great Georgian metropolis was home to hundreds of lodgers.

The 'uninhabited' houses were not differentiated into those that were ruinous and those that were being built. This distinction was noted and would be acted upon for the 1811 census.

Surviving censuses taken at the time of the national censuses and those taken for other local purposes are detailed in the guides of Gibson and Medlycott, and Chapman. A more recent guide has been put together by Richard Wall, Matthew Woollard and Beatrice Moring of the University of Essex and can be read online. *Census Schedules and Listings, 1801–1831: An Introduction and Guide* (University of Essex, 2004) is at **www.essex. ac.uk/history/Staff_Research/working-papers/MW-RW-BM.pdf**.

The 1831 census (as sent to the government) has been digitized by Staffordshire University. The 1831 census database can be accessed at **www.staffs.ac.uk/schools/humanities_and_soc_sciences/census/cen1831.htm**. A transcription of the 1831 census of County Londonderry is available to download from **www.billmacafee.com**.

The 1801, 1811, 1821 and 1831 censuses for some parishes in the following counties of England, Wales, Scotland, and for Ireland (for 1821 and 1831 only) survive as listed here. You should find the following records at the relevant local record offices or libraries:

	1801	1811	1821	1831
Bedfordshire		•	•	•
Berkshire	•	•	•	
Buckinghamshire			•	•
Cambridgeshire		•	•	•
Cheshire		•	•	•
Cornwall	•	•	•	
Cumberland		•	•	•
Derbyshire	•	•	•	•
Devon	•	•	•	•
Dorset	•	•	•	•
County Durham			•	
Essex	•	•	•	•
Gloucestershire and Bristol	•	•	•	•
Hampshire	•	•	•	•
Herefordshire	•	•		•
Hertfordshire	•		•	
Huntingdonshire		•	•	
Kent	•	•	•	•
Lancashire	•	•	•	•
Leicestershire	•	•	•	•
Lincolnshire	•	•	•	•
Norfolk	•	•	•	•
Northamptonshire		•	•	
Northumberland		•	•	
Nottinghamshire	•	•	•	•
Oxfordshire	•	•	•	•
Shropshire	•		•	•
Somerset	•	•	•	•
Staffordshire	•	•	•	•
Suffolk	•	•	•	•

	1801	1811	1821	1831
Surrey	•	•	•	•
Sussex	•	•	•	•
Warwickshire	•	•	•	•
Westmoreland	•	•		
Wiltshire	•	•	•	•
Worcestershire		•	•	•
York	•	•	•	
North Riding of Yorkshire		•	•	
West Riding of Yorkshire	•	•	•	•
East Riding of Yorkshire	•	•	•	•
Anglesey	•		•	
Cardiganshire			•	
Carmarthenshire			•	
Denbighshire		•	•	
Flintshire		•	•	•
Montgomeryshire			•	
Guernsey			•	
Aberdeenshire	•			
Angus (Forfarshire)	•	•		
Ayrshire	•	•	•	•
Banffshire			•	
Berwickshire		•		•
Dumfriesshire	•	•	•	
Fife			•	
Inverness-shire	•		•	•
Kincardineshire		•	•	
Kirkcudbrightshire			•	•
Lanarkshire			•	
Midlothian	•	•	•	•
Moray (Elginshire)		•		
Orkney			•	
Peeblesshire	•			
Perthshire		•	•	•
Renfrewshire			•	
Roxburghshire				•
Shetland			•	
Strathclyde			•	
Sutherland		•		
Armagh			•	
Cavan			•	

	1801	1811	1821	1831
Dublin				•
Fermanagh			•	
Galway			•	
Kerry			•	
Kilkenny			•	•
King's County (Offaly)			•	
Leitrim			•	
Londonderry				•
Meath			•	
Tipperary			•	
Waterford			•	

For Ireland, records survive on microfilm at the National Archives of Ireland (NAI) for

Cavan, Ireland	31 parishes
Fermanagh	2 parishes
Galway	9 parishes (incomplete)
King's County (Offaly)	9 parishes
Meath	19 parishes (incomplete)

Transcripts are now available online at the National Archives of Ireland website: **http://www.census.nationalarchives.ie/**

London and Middlesex, by far the most highly populated areas of the UK in this period, are very well covered with named censuses as follows:

	1801	1811	1821	1831
St Helen's, Bishopgate	•		•	
St Nicholas, Acons	•	•	•	•
St Sepulchre, Holborn	•	•	•	
Allhallows, Lombard Street		•	•	
St Benet Paul's Wharf		•	•	
St Benet Sherehog		•	•	
St Mary Woolchurch Haw		•	•	•
St Mary Woolnoth		•	•	•
St Peter Cornhill		•	•	•
St Peter Paul's Wharf		•		•
St Swithin London Stone with St Mary Bothaw		•	•	
St Thomas Apostle		•	•	•

	1801	1811	1821	1831
St Ann Blackfriars	•			
St Margaret, Lothbury			•	•
St Margaret, Abchurch			•	•
St Katherine Coleman			•	•
St Botolph, Bishopsgate	•			
St John the Baptist, Walbrook	•			
St Christopher le Stocks				•
St Clement, Eastcheap				•
St Kathleen Cree				•
St Matthew Friday Street				•
St Peter Westcheap				•
St John at Hackney		•	•	•
Hampstead	•	•		
Hammersmith			•	•
Harrow				•
Hendon	•	•	•	
Westminster St Margaret	•	•	•	
Westminster St Mary le Strand	•	•	•	
Chelsea St Luke	•			
Chiswick	•			
Little Stanmore				•
St Marylebone			•	•
St James Piccadilly	•			
Poplar All Saints			•	•
Willesden			•	•

Local Censuses 1801–31 Online

Increasingly, transcripts of these local censuses of 1801–31 have been digitized. Transcripts of the following local censuses can currently be searched. Not all contain names. A useful overview of the census online can be found at **www.genuki.org.uk/big/eng/Census.html**:

Census Year	Census Place	Web Address
1801	Amlwch, Anglesey	**www.genuki.org.uk/big/wal/AGY/ Amlwch/Amlwch1801.html**
1801	Baconsthorpe, Norfolk	**www.origins.org.uk/genuki/NFK/ places/b/baconsthorpe/census1801. shtml**

Census Year	Census Place	Web Address
1801	Beeston (with Bittering), Norfolk	www.origins.org.uk/genuki/NFK/ places/b/ beeston/census1801.shtml
1801	Hethersett, Norfolk	www.origins.org.uk/genuki/NFK/ places/h/hethersett/census1801. shtml
1801	Illington, Norfolk	www.origins.org.uk/genuki/NFK/ places/i/ illington/census1801.shtml
1801	Ingworth, Norfolk	www.origins.org.uk/genuki/NFK/ places/i/ingworth/census1801.shtml
1801	Weston Longville, Norfolk	www.origins.org.uk/genuki/ NFK/places/w/weston_ longville/ census1801.shtml
1801	Winfarthing, Norfolk	www.origins.org.uk/genuki/NFK/ places/w/winfarthing/census1801. shtml
1801	Woodton, Norfolk	www.origins.org.uk/genuki/NFK/ places/w/woodton/census1801. shtml
1801	Huntspill, Somerset	http://www.durtnall.org.uk/ Huntspill/CENSUS.htm
1801	Southill Broom and Bedfordshire	http://bedsarchives.bedford.gov.uk/ Guide-to-Collections/FamilyHistory/ SouthillBroomandStanford1801 Census.aspx
1801	Bickleigh (near Tiverton), Devon	https://www.genuki.org.uk/big/ eng/DEV/bickleighT/bickleighT 1801
1801	Mortehoe, Devon	https://www.genuki.org.uk/big/ eng/DEV/Mortehoe/Mortehoe1801
1801	Dundee, Forfarshire	www.fdca.org.uk/pdf%20files/1801 CensusT.pdf
1801	Dundee, Forfarshire	www.fdca.org.uk/Burgh_Records. html
1811	Hope, Derbyshire	http://freepages.rootsweb.com/~ dusk/genealogy/1811_hope/1811_ hope.html
1811	Honley, West Yorkshire	http://freepages.rootsweb.com/ ~honleycemetery/genealogy/ census.htm

Census Year	Census Place	Web Address
1811	Calverley and Farsley, West Yorkshire	http://www.calverley.info/cen_1811.htm
1811	Tong, West Yorkshire	http://www.tong.calverley.info/1811.html
1811	Whitchurch, Dorset	www.opcdorset.org/WhCanonicorum Files/1811WhCanonicorum.htm
1811	Corfe Castle, Dorset	www.opcdorset.org/CorfeCastle Files/1811CorfeCastle.htm
1811	Baconsthorpe, Norfolk	www.origins.org.uk/genuki/NFK/places/b/baconsthorpe/census1811.shtml
1811	Great Bircham, Norfolk	www.origins.org.uk/genuki/NFK/places/b/bircham_great/census1811.shtml
1811	Old Buckenham, Norfolk	www.origins.org.uk/genuki/NFK/places/b/buckenham_old/census1811.shtml
1811	Winfarthing, Norfolk	www.origins.org.uk/genuki/NFK/places/w/winfarthing/census1811.shtml
1811	Wacton, Norfolk	www.origins.org.uk/genuki/NFK/places/w/wacton/census1811.shtml
1811	Lower Hardres Canterbury, Kent	http://members.multimania.co.uk/elmsted/census/lhardres1811.htm
1811	Mossley, Lancashire	www.tamesidefamilyhistory.co.uk/1811censusmossley.htm
1811	Stalybridge, Lancashire	www.tamesidefamilyhistory.co.uk/1811censusstalybridge1.htm
1811	Dallas, Moray	http://www.wakefieldfhs.org.uk/morayweb/Dallas%201811%20Census.htm
1821	Axminster, Devon	https://www.genuki.org.uk/big/eng/DEV/Axminster/Axminster1821
1821	Bickleigh near near Tiverton), Devon	https://www.genuki.org.uk/big/eng/DEV/BickleighT/BickleighT1821
1821	Cheriton Bishop, Devon	https://www.genuki.org.uk/big/eng/DEV/CheritonBishop/CheritonBishop1821

Census Year	Census Place	Web Address
1821	Dean Prior, Devon	https://www.genuki.org.uk/big/ eng/DEV/DeanPrior/DeanPrior 1821
1821	Dunsford, Devon	https://www.genuki.org.uk/big/ eng/DEV/Dunsford/Dunsford1821
1821	Exeter Holy Trinity, Devon	https://www.genuki.org.uk/big eng/DEV/Exeter/HolyTrinity/Holy Trinity1821
1821	Tedburn St Mary, Devon	https://www.genuki.org.uk /big/eng/DEV/TedburnStMary/ TedburnStMary1821
1821	St Hilary, Cornwall	https://www.genuki.org.uk/big/ eng/CON/StHilary#Census
1821	Veryan, Cornwall	http://freepages.genealogy.roots web.ancestry. com/~dtrounce/ veryanlists.html
1821	Marnhull, Dorset	www.opcdorset.org/MarnhullFiles/ 1821Marnhull.htm
1821	Corfe Castle, Dorset	www.opcdorset.org/CorfeCastleFiles/ 1821CorfeCastle.htm
1821	Whitchurch, Dorset	www.opcdorset.org/ WinterborneFiles/W.Whitchurch/ 1821WinterborneWhitechurch.htm
1821	Baconsthorpe, Norfolk	www.origins.org.uk/genuki/NFK places/b/baconsthorpe/census1821. shtml
1821	Dunston, Norfolk	www.origins.org.uk/genuki/NFK/ places/d/dunston/census1821. shtml
1821	Bodham, Norfolk	https://www.genuki.org.uk/big/ eng/NFK/Bodham/Census1821
1821	Bradfield, Norfolk	www.origins.org.uk/genuki/NFK/ places/b/bradfield/census1821. shtml
1821	Old Buckenham, Norfolk	www.origins.org.uk/genuki/NFK/ places/b/buckenham_old/census 1821.shtml
1821	Tuttington, Norfolk	www.origins.org.uk/genuki/NFK/ places/t/tuttington/census1821. shtml

Census Year	Census Place	Web Address
1821	Winfarthing, Norfolk	www.origins.org.uk/genuki/NFK/places/w/winfarthing/census1821.shtml
1821	Hayes, Kent	http://freepages.genealogy.rootsweb.ancestry.com/~mrawson/1821indx.html
1821	Tong, West Yorkshire	www.calverley.info/cen_tong_1821.htm
1831	St Hilary, Cornwall	http://opc-cornwall.org/Records/parishes/H-K/hilary_st_census_1831.php
1831	Allington, Dorset	http://www.opcdorset.org/Allington_Bridport/Allington/1831Allington.htm
1831	Corfe Castle, Dorset	www.opcdorset.org/CorfeCastleFiles/1831/CorfeCastle.htm
1831	Ryme Intrinseca, Dorset	http://www.opcdorset.org/RymeIntrinsecaFiles/RymeIntrinsecaCensus1831.htm
1831	Alderford, Norfolk	www.origins.org.uk/genuki/NFK/places/a/alderford/census1831.shtml
1831	Coston, Norfolk	www.origins.org.uk/genuki/NFK/places/c/coston/census1831.shtml
1831	Sheffield, West Riding of Yorkshire	www.findmypast.co.uk/search/other-records/nether-hallam-census
1831	Jedburgh, Roxburghshire	https://www.scottishindexes.com ecsearch.aspx/

Census Alternatives

Besides censuses, other types of population records were created before 1841. As well as the religious censuses that were taken across Britain and Ireland, family historians can explore Easter books, communicants' lists, and the church incumbents' visiting books that were kept between 1587 and 1891. Family historians often use records like these as alternatives to censuses, especially where no other population listings survive. Some of the records have been compiled into books, whereas others need to be examined in person at the relevant archive. These archives can be identified through The National Archives' Discovery catalogue **https://discovery.nationalarchives.gov.uk/**

CORNWALL ONLINE PARISH CLERKS - helping bring the past alive			

Return to St Hilary Parish Page

St Hilary - 1821 Census

A census of the Population of the Parish of St Hilary independently of the Town & vicinity of Marazion taken on the 28th & 29th of May 1821 by Mr. Wm. Richards, churchwarden during the incumbancy of the Revd. Thomas Pascoe.

By Order of Parliament

Question				Number & age of	Males	Females
1	Inhabited houses	168		Under 5 years	131	129
	Total number of families	292		From 5 to 10	92	101
2	Houses now building	3		From 10 to 15	133	81
3	Un-inhabited houses	6		From 15 to 20	77	77
4	Number of families chiefly employed in agriculture			From 20 to 30	131	122
		113				
	Manufacturers or handicrafts			From 30 to 40	74	94
	Not comprised in the two preceeding classes. N.B. the principal part of these are miners.					
				From 40 to 50	55	66
				From 50 to 60	39	45
				From 60 to 70	27	37
		179		From 70 to 80	11	19
5	No. of males	775		From 80 to 90	4	11
	No. of females	783		From 90 to 100	1	1
	Total number		1558	Total	775	783

Screenshot of the Cornwall Online Parish Clerks website showing the entries for the 1821 census of St Hilary (https://www.opc-cornwall.org/Records/parishes/H-K/hilary_ st_census_1821.php)

An example of one book that can be seen at larger libraries is A. Dyer and D.M. Palliser, *The Diocesan Population Returns for 1563 and 1603* (in the 'Records of Social and Economic History' series, Oxford University Press, 2005).

In March 1766, the Irish House of Lords ordered the Church of Ireland to compile returns of the heads of households in their parishes. This was done in March and April of that year. The consequent returns were destroyed in 1922, but surviving transcripts were made. From these are formed the records of the 1766 Religious Census of Ireland. The fragments are held at the Public Record Office of Northern Ireland (PRONI), but the transcripts are available to view on the Ancestry website.

Other useful census alternatives for Ireland include:

- 1521–1603 Fiants (published volumes: *The Irish Fiants of the Tudor sovereigns during the reigns of Henry VIII, Edward VI, Philip and Mary, Elizabeth I*, Edmund Burke, 1994)
- 1630 muster rolls (published by county, available at PRONI)
- 1641 books of survey and distribution (manuscripts at the National Library; published volumes for Clare, Galway, Mayo and Roscommon, Irish Manuscripts Commission)

- 1646–56 civil survey (volumes on the twelve surviving counties of Cork, Derry, Donegal, Dublin, Kildare, Kilkenny, Limerick, Meath, Tipperary, Tyrone, Waterford and Wexford, Irish Manuscripts Commission)
- 1664 hearth tax (surviving hearth money rolls at PRONI, lists are by county).

Militia lists and musters taken across the centuries for various parts of Britain have often been used as census substitutes. Militia were raised, primarily for home defence, from local able-bodied men, but they could be called upon in times of war. Local recruitment officers (often parish officials) drew up lists of eligible men. These lists included names, and could also mention infirmities, occupations, numbers of children and ages. Records of the militia lists and musters are held at TNA and local record offices. Some lists are featured in the guides of Gibson and Medlycott, and Chapman.

As Simon Fowler writes in *Digging Deeper* (p.130),

> the system was reformed during the Seven Years War in 1757. The militia became particularly important during the Napoleonic wars, when invasion was expected several times. Men between the ages of 18 and 45 could be called up for service by ballot, although you could get out of service by finding a substitute to fill your place. Each parish was required to provide lists of men who could serve in the militia. There were some exceptions, including clergymen, apprentices, articled clerks and former soldiers and sailors, even so David Hey says that the returns 'provide the best occupational census returns that is available before … the nineteenth century'.

The militia and militia enrolment lists of 1758 to 1831 can thus be used as alternative censuses for males aged 18 to 45 in this period.

Ratebooks in England and Wales can provide a useful alternative to censuses in the years in between national censuses and for those prior to 1841. The books give the names of the ratepayers and sometimes the owners of each property in the area of administration. Where they survive, these books are usually held at local archives or record offices. Some have been microfilmed. Similarly, street and trade directories record the names and addresses of those who paid to be included in them. They are particularly useful for tracing ancestors involved in trade or public houses.

For Scotland, communion rolls name adult males of a particular church. They are thus less useful for identifying all inhabitants of a given parish. The communion rolls can be viewed through digital images at the National Records of Scotland.

Between 1910 and 1915, the Valuation Office made a survey of land valuation for purposes of duty under the Finance Act of 1909–10. This became known as the Lloyd George 'Domesday' Survey, after the Chancellor of the Exchequer who introduced the bill. In 1910, the first major records created as part of the survey were the valuation books (also known as 'Domesday books'). The books include the name of the owner, the map reference of the property, the occupier of the property, the situation, description and extent. They can be a useful alternative to censuses when researching the history of properties. Surviving valuation books are held in reference IR 91 at TNA (for the City of London and the City of Westminster) and local archives.

Census Alternatives Online

Results of the 1676 Bishop Compton census can be found in the digital library, British History Online, at **www.british-history.ac.uk**.

Transcriptions of Pender's Census of 1659 can be read at **http:// clanmaclochlainn.com/1659cen.htm**. Some images of this census for Armagh can be seen at **www.igp-web.com**

William Morton Pitt's 1790 census of Corfe Castle and District, Dorset (transcribed by the Dorset Family History Society, www.dorsetfhs.org. uk) can be explored at **www.findmypast.co.uk/search/other-records/ corfe-castle-census**

In c.1830, the Dromore Presbyterian Church took a religious census of its congregation in County Tyrone. Almost 700 members of the parish are named, including children. Copies of the original census have been microfilmed and are held at PRONI, ref. MIC 1P/247a. The census has been transcribed to the Emerald Ancestors website at **www. emeraldancestors.com**

One of the most commonly used census substitutes are the records of the hearth tax. From 1662 to 1689, this tax was levied on each householder according to the number of hearths in their abode. The surviving records are held at The National Archives, ref. E 179. Some lists of names can be downloaded from **www.hearthtax.org.uk**

Ancestry holds records of the Land Tax Redemption of 1798. These can act as a census alternative as they reveal names of home-owners and tenants (heads of household) across the country. They do not give details of other family members, but they do provide the value of the property.

The Irish tithe applotment books of 1823–38 have been microfilmed by the LDS. Of these, the following have been transcribed online:

- Armagh: **www.connorsgenealogy.com/Armagh/BallymoreTithes-AB.htm**
- Carlow: **http://www.from-ireland.net/tithe-apployment-book-barragh-carlow/**
- Clare: **http://titheapplotmentbooks.nationalarchives.ie/pagestab/Clare/Kilkeedy/**
- Cork: **http://titheapplotmentbooks.nationalarchives.ie/pagestab/Cork/** and **www.bandon-genealogy.com/kilbrogan-tithes.htm**

Between 1848 and 1864, a survey of Ireland was taken that is now known as Griffith's Valuation. This valuation was intended to determine who was liable to pay the poor law rates. It lists all occupiers of land, tenements and houses. Original and printed volumes are held at PRONI, but transcriptions are available online at Findmypast **https://search.findmypast.co.uk/search-world-records/griffiths-valuation-1847-1864** and **www.askaboutireland.ie**

Lists of English and Welsh landowners of 1873, Scottish landowners of 1872–3 and Irish landowners of 1876 can be searched at TheGenealogist website.

Colonial Censuses

Britain's imperialists used censuses and other population surveys to aid their rule in the colonies and protectorates of the empire. The British government tried to extend the national census of 1861 to include the empire but results did not prove complete or accurate. The report on this can be viewed on HISTPOP. Earlier surviving census returns of the former colonies should be held in their respective national archives.

Besides these, there are a small number of colonial censuses in the collections of TNA. They include:

1715	Census of the white population of Barbados (TNA ref. CO 28/16).
1787–1859	Censuses of convicts (and some free settlers) in New South Wales and Tasmania (ref. HO 10). The most complete is the 1828 census of New South Wales (ref. HO 10/21–27). This has been published in Malcolm R. Sainty and Keith A. Johnson (eds), *Census of New South Wales, November 1828* (Library of Australian History, 1980).
1811	Surinam (contains names of slaves, as well as free black and white inhabitants) (ref. CO 278/15–25).
1831 (30 June)	Census of Sierra Leone (ref. CO 267/111).

Of the Dominions, regular censuses were taken in Australia and New Zealand but most were destroyed. A name index to the surviving parts of the 1841 census of New South Wales can be searched at **www.records.nsw. gov.au/state-archives/indexes-online/indexes-online**. Surviving parts of the Tasmanian censuses of 1837, 1838, 1842, 1843, 1848, 1851 and 1857 have been digitized. Indexes can be searched and images viewed at **https://ctfl. libraries.tas.gov.au/menu.aspx?search=8**

In Canada, census records from 1851 have been archived at the Library and Archives Canada and have been digitized. These records can be explored via **https://www.bac-lac.gc.ca/eng/census/1851/Pages/1851.aspx**. Surviving parts of the 1666–1901 censuses can also be searched on microfilm at the library.

Chapter 3

1841: THE FIRST MODERN CENSUS

Historical Context

KEY EVENTS OF 1831–1841

- 1832: Representation of the People Act (Reform Act)
- 1836: Creation of the General Register Office; first Registrar General appointed: Thomas Lister
- 1837: A new queen ascends to the throne, heralding the Victorian Age
- Chartism reaches its height
- 1841: Sir Robert Peel succeeds William Lamb, 2nd Viscount Melbourne as prime minister of the United Kingdom.

The census revealed the population of Great Britain and Ireland to be 18,553,124.

John Rickman, the statistician who conducted the first four censuses, died in 1840. With Rickman's death, the census moved into a new era. Hangovers from the Georgian period were still present, such as the Whig Prime Minister Lord Melbourne, who had been in office since 1835, following a first term in 1834. Social and political changes highlighted the need for a more efficient census to make sense of the modern era. Britain was at the tail end of its Industrial Revolution. Technical innovations, industrial development and large-scale urbanization proved the mainspring of socio-economic change. Politicians, religious leaders, teachers and social commentators were becoming concerned with the welfare of the enlarged urban population.

Epidemiologists and other doctors developed theories of disease being caused by the miasma or 'bad air' of the growing towns and cities. Edwin Chadwick, the leading proponent of public health reform in

Victorian Britain, developed the 'sanitary principle' in which he argued that it was insanitary living conditions that caused 'the various forms of epidemic, endemic, and other diseases' and that they were 'aggravated, or propagated chiefly among the labouring classes by atmospheric impurities produced by decomposing animal and vegetable substances, by damp and filth, and close and overcrowded dwellings'.[1] The census of 1841 would be used to establish the extent to which the urban slums were overcrowded. Chadwick also identified workers in certain occupations, such as sewer cleaners, who, he argued, were more vulnerable to disease. The occupational statistics in this census would be used to support this theory.

In among the Reform Act and other Whig reforms, the 1830s and 1840s saw the height of Chartism, a radical working-class movement for political reform. Now, more than earlier in the century, the Establishment began to feel threatened by members of the working classes. Not only were there pockets of radicalism among the working classes, but their numbers were higher. Since 1801, the population had almost doubled. The Establishment needed to take control of the growing working class, and to establish who they were and how they lived. This would be achieved, in part, through a new form of census. However, this census was not without its problems.

In 1841, there was a radical change in the compilation of the census. It is significant to family historians as it was the first to list the names of every individual in a household. This change was introduced after suggestions made by members of the London Statistical Society that were incorporated into the Population Act of 1840 (3 & 4 Vict., c. 99). These included naming individuals and noting their details on household schedules, using transcripts of the local enumerators to collate each household's details, and tabulating all the data in one place. The Population Act also created the post of Registrar General of England and Wales. For genealogists, therefore, the 1841 census is seen as the first useful and comprehensive census for UK research; the first to name every individual and to record personal information across all areas, and the first to survive (almost) in its entirety.

The first Registrar General was Thomas Henry Lister (1800–42), a sometime-romantic novelist,[2] who had been appointed in 1836 with the creation of the General Register Office (GRO). He established the system of civil registration of births, marriages and deaths (Marriage Act of 1836: 6 & 7 Wm IV, c 85, and the Births and Deaths Registration Act of 1836: 6 & 7 Wm IV, c 86). The 1840 Population Act (based on a bill drafted by Lister) resulted in Lister being appointed as the first commissioner responsible for organizing the count of the new census. Later two other commissioners were appointed: the Hon. Edmund Phipps and Thomas Vardon, the librarian of the House of Commons. For the first time, the administration of the census would take place at the General Register Office, and counting would be done by local officers of the new census registration districts. As Registrar General, Thomas Lister would be in charge of the census process. At this stage, the GRO was under the control of the Home Office; hence The National Archives' (formerly the Public Record Office) reference for the census records is HO.

The Home Office also oversaw census-taking in Scotland for this year, although the sheriff substitute of each Scottish county aided the process locally. In Ireland, three census commissioners were appointed to oversee the process: William Tighe Hamilton, Henry Brownrigg and Thomas Aiskew Larcom. Of these, Larcom (1801–79) is seen by historians as being the most significant. It was he who wrote in the *Report of the commissioners appointed to take the census of Ireland for the year 1841*, p.vi, 'We felt, in fact, that a Census ought to be Social Survey, not a bare enumeration.'[3] This was a key change for the census of the UK as a whole at this point: organizers wanted to acquire a deeper and fuller picture of society at this time. A new development in Ireland was that householders themselves could fill in the schedules; previously, they were all completed by enumerators. In this year, most enumerators were policemen, overseen by Census Commissioner Henry Brownrigg, who also served as Inspector General of the Constabulary.

The census registration districts of 1841 were based on those used for civil registration, which were based in turn on the poor law unions and were not matched exactly to parish boundaries. Some fitted existing parishes, but the biggest complication for researchers today is that the new districts crossed county boundaries. The registrars divided their sub-districts into smaller districts that would be administered by temporary enumerators. These enumerators were appointed by the local registrars. The Act had stipulated that overseers of the poor, relieving officers, constables or other peace officers (i.e. those who enforced the law) were bound to act as enumerators, if required by the commissioners. Lister did not want householders to complete household schedules as he feared most were too illiterate to do so. He was persuaded by a trial census in London which showed the high number of enumerators that would be needed to collect the information by knocking on doors. To legitimize the use of schedules, a second Act (4 & 5 Vict., c. 7) was passed at short notice on 6 April 1841. The enumerators were given instruction booklets detailing their role. Examples of these are held at TNA, ref. RG 27/1. In the week leading up to census night, the enumerators gave each household in England, Wales, Scotland, the Channel Islands and the Isle of Man a blank form (or 'schedule') asking for the name, age, gender, occupation and address of those sleeping at the property on the night of Sunday, 6 June 1841. In the event, the addresses given were often simply the names of the village or road, rather than exact residences. The census was intended to include any persons working away that night who would be returning in the morning. However, this was to become an area of confusion and led to some people being listed twice, while others were not listed at all.

An additional problem was the spelling of names, especially surnames, by those unable to read or write. Nowadays, most names can be identified using spelling-variant options on online census databases, but some were badly transcribed and bear no resemblance to the actual name.

The census schedules have since been destroyed, but most of their details remain in the enumerators' books, where they were copied. The enumerator wrote up all the details of the completed householders' schedules in the census enumerators' book (CEB). These documents were then sent to the district registrar, who checked them before forwarding them

1841 Census of Herm (Ref. HO 107/146021/1, p. 1). (© Crown Copyright Images reproduced by courtesy of The National Archives, London, England. www.NationalArchives.gov.uk & www.TheGenealogist.co.uk)

on to the census office, which was based in the General Register Office in London. It was here that the schedules were subsequently destroyed. The CEBs were retained and used for statistical purposes. It is these that have been digitized and which family historians use in their research today. The reports included population tables that can be seen at HISTPOP.

Enumerators had different experiences depending on the area covered. On Monday, 7 June, most rose at sunrise to begin collecting the completed schedules. They returned them to the local registrars the following day. The enumerators were paid, but many considered their remuneration inadequate. In Ireland, confusion over payment led to an over-counting of the population as some enumerators believed they were paid per head. Confusion and poor preparation for the census led to a great variation in the quality of the enumerators. Many whom the registrars deemed suitable for the task were not keen to participate. In Scotland, most enumerators on this census were schoolmasters. Across England and Wales, too, many schoolmasters were employed, although others were local farmers or craftsmen.

What Details are Included?

The census enumerators' books (CEBs) requested the following:[4]

Page i: Geographical information – both ancient divisions (county, hundred, parish, etc.) and those for registration purposes (superintendent registrar's district, registrar's district, number of enumeration district). Description of enumeration district.

Page ii: Blank.

Page iii: Extract from Census Act regarding the penalty for refusing information or giving false answers.

Page iv: Directions for filling up the book.

Page v: Example of how to fill up the book.

Pages 1–x: Pages for the insertion of nominal information, numbered 1 to x.

First page: Summary table of the total number of houses and persons in each of the foregoing pages.

Second page: Summary tables regarding itinerants, the temporary increase and decrease of the population, and emigration.

Third page: Declarations signed by the enumerators, registrar and superintendent registrar.

The headings on the household schedules are:

- PLACE
- HOUSES
  Uninhabited or Building Inhabited
- NAMES OF EACH PERSON WHO ABODE THEREIN THE PRECEDING NIGHT
- AGE AND SEX
  Male
  Female
- PROFESSION, TRADE, EMPLOYMENT, OR OF INDEPENDENT MEANS
- WHERE BORN
  Whether Born in same County
  Whether Born in Scotland, Ireland, or Foreign Parts.

At the top of each schedule the enumerator was required to state the name of the city or borough, and parish or township. The response to whether born in the same county was to be completed as 'Y' or 'N' for yes or no. For 'Whether born in Scotland, Ireland or Foreign parts', the response was instructed to be 'S', 'I' or 'F'.

Besides these, the enumerators had to complete summary tables, which asked for the following:

- Number of males and females in vessels on inland navigable waters, in mines or pits, in barns or sheds, in tents or in the open air, or not enumerated as inmates of any dwelling house
- The probable number of males and females temporarily present or temporarily absent from the district, and the cause thereof
- Number of persons emigrated to the colonies or foreign countries since 31 December 1840.

The enumerators were expected to give an account of individuals in their district who slept on the night of 6 June 'in barges, boats, or other small vessels, remaining stationary on canals or other inland navigable waters; in mines or pits; in barns, sheds, or the like; in tents or in the open air; and all not enumerated (although abiding within the district) as inmates of any dwelling-house from other causes'.

The addresses recorded were usually basic, with only a street or village name, although large houses and inns may be noted.

Although enumerators were required to note the age of each individual, these were rounded down to the nearest five for persons over the age of 15. It is important to note that in some cases the exact age was recorded, and in others confusion led to the age being rounded *up* to the nearest five.

When it came to the question of whether the resident was born in the county where the census took place, many mistakes were made with this question. A 'Y' or 'Yes' in the response column is not always proof that your ancestor was born in the county.

As a disincentive to inaccurate returns, superintendent-registrars, registrars or enumerators who made wilfully false declarations could be penalized between 40s and £5. In 2005, the £5 of 1840 would be worth around £220.[5]

Finding Aids

Indexes exist for the census on all the website providers (see below).

The National Archives series code for this census is HO 107. The pieces are arranged by registration district (RD). Where the registration district is not known, check *Register of towns indexed by streets for the 1841–1881 census of England and Wales* (LDS Family History Library Catalog number 6026692). The folio number was stamped in the upper-right corner of the right-side page.

Indexes have been produced by a number of family history societies, such as the *Huddersfield township census return A-Z index. 1841 Census: Huddersfield Township Mi-Re*, Part 7 of 10 by Dr David Allen Sykes and Stephen David Whitwam (Huddersfield and District FHS, 1994). Some of these are available via their respective websites. Others are in book form or on CD-ROM.

As a result of its new features and confusion over certain aspects, the 1841 census can be difficult to use when searching for ancestors. The vagaries of trying to find an ancestor, for example, with a common name like David Jones and of an uncertain age (as age varies in later censuses) in Wales, when the birthplace reveals only that he was born or not born in the county in which he is living, can prove challenging. Many individuals who were born outside the county are marked with a 'Y', and vice versa, often rendering the results in this column highly unreliable. Besides the vague details revealed, so many parts of this census have faded that a lot of names are unrecognizable. When searching, it is worth checking the names you find on the census against censuses for other years, and against other genealogical sources, such as the English and Welsh birth, marriage and death civil registration indexes on **www.freebmd.org.uk** in order to confirm the original name or identity of your ancestors.

Some errors have been made in transcriptions by the various providers of online censuses, and it is useful to try searches on different sites.

As with the later censuses, missing ancestors may be recorded in the CEBs under different names. An illegitimate child, for example, may be found on the census under the name of the householder or stepparent. There is also the possibility of enumerator error: surnames and birthplaces are often mistranscribed by the use of 'ditto' (to indicate repetition of the entry above), often written as 'Do' or with the '"' mark.

Online Resources

The 1841 census indexes, transcriptions and images for England, Wales, the Channel Islands and the Isle of Man are included on commercial data provider sites: Ancestry, UK Census Online, TheGenealogist, Genes Reunited, Findmypast and RootsUK. FamilySearch offers free access to an index and transcriptions for this year, with a link to view images at the commercial Findmypast website. Free data is also available at FreeCEN.

Indexes and brief transcriptions for the Scottish 1841 census can be viewed on FamilySearch, Ancestry, Genes Reunited and Findmypast. The only website to give full access to the images of the Scottish censuses is ScotlandsPeople.

Some census transcriptions are available on Scottish Indexes.

Free Resources

The English and Welsh censuses can be searched for free at many archives across Britain. These include The National Archives, National Library of Wales, Society of Genealogists, London Metropolitan Archives, most county record offices and many local libraries. The Scottish censuses can be searched at the ScotlandsPeople Centre, the Mitchell Library and other family history centres.

The indexes on the online census databases are free to search, but there is usually a charge to view documents.

Currently the FreeCen website of UK census transcriptions, **www. freecen.org.uk**, provides free access to 1841 census data for some parishes in the following counties:

Cornwall	Nottinghamshire	Ayrshire
Devon	Somerset	Banffshire
Dorset	Warwickshire	Berwickshire
Gloucestershire	Wiltshire	Bute
Huntingdonshire	Aberdeenshire	Caithness
Lincolnshire	Angus (Forfarshire)	Clackmannanshire
Middlesex	Argyllshire	Dumfriesshire

Dunbartonshire	Midlothian	Roxburghshire
East Lothian	Morayshire	Selkirkshire
Fife	Nairnshire	Shetland Isles
Inverness-shire	Orkney Isles	Stirlingshire
Kincardineshire	Peeblesshire	Sutherland
Kinross-shire	Perthshire	West Lothian
Kirkcudbright	Renfrewshire	Wigtownshire
Lanarkshire	Ross & Cromarty	

Many of the online parish clerk (OPC) websites for specific counties give transcriptions of the 1841 census for certain parishes in their locality.

Transcriptions for 1841 are freely available for England, Wales, Isle of Man and Channel Islands on the FamilySearch website. Images can be browsed. All Scottish transcriptions are available.

Problems

Sunday, 6 June 1841 was a harvest night. The weather was fine, and good for making hay. For this reason, agricultural labourer ancestors ('ag labs') may be missing from the census if they were sleeping outside, or

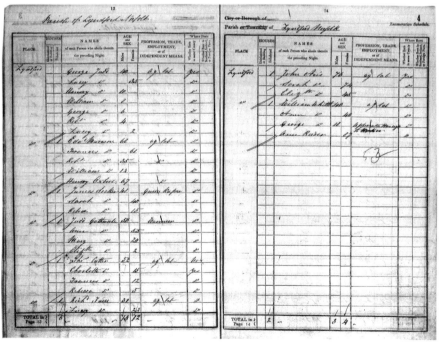

1841 Census entry for Henry Oxboro (Ref. HO 107/774/8/17/3 p. 13). (© Crown Copyright Images reproduced by courtesy of The National Archives, London, England. www.NationalArchives.gov.uk & www.TheGenealogist.co.uk)

were located away from home, maybe in a neighbouring village near where they were working. According to the enumerators' instructions, agricultural labourers 'may include all farming servants and labourers in husbandry'. The area around Ascot racecourse saw more residents than usual as the 6th was a race day.

The surname 'Oxborough' had a number of variants, and this illiterate family appears in records under different spellings, including 'Oxboro', 'Oxburgh' and 'Oxborow'. The previous image from the schedule of the hamlet of Lynford in Norfolk shows 67-year-old agricultural labourer, Henry Oxboro, residing with the household of fellow labourer, 68-year-old Edward Morrison. We know from other sources that Henry lived in the neighbouring village of Mundford, where his wife, Susan, and daughter, Ann Pymar, are shown as residing on census night. Henry's presence in Lynford suggests he has been working on the harvest there. All the 1,100 acres of land in Lynford were owned by Sir Richard Sutton, Baronet.

Other workers who are missing from the census include seamen working offshore, who were not enumerated, although a count was made of the total number of merchant seaman for the report. No census was taken of members of the armed forces outside the UK. Those in

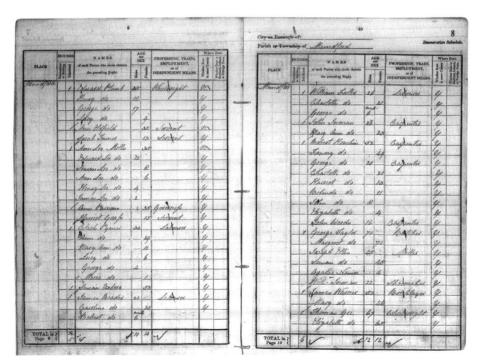

1841 Census entry for Susan Oxboro (Ref. HO 107/774/10/16/8 p. 9). (© Crown Copyright Images reproduced by courtesy of The National Archives, London, England. www.NationalArchives.gov.uk & www.TheGenealogist.co.uk)

England and Wales were not enumerated separately. A count was taken of members of the Royal Navy aboard ship and this is found in the report.

Others were enumerated but their schedules were subsequently lost or destroyed. The census returns for the Fife parishes of Abdie, Auchtermuchty, Balmerino, Ceres, Collessie, Creich, Cults, Cupar, Dairsie, Dunbog, Kinghorn, Kinglassie, Kirkcaldy and Leslie were all lost when the ferryboat that was carrying them sank in the Forth estuary en route to Edinburgh. Other parishes, such as Arngask, Burntisland and Kennoway, also have books missing.

Original 1841 census returns in London were also lost in transit from Kensington, Paddington, Golden Lane and Whitecross in Finsbury St Luke.

In order to identify exactly which parishes are missing from this census, search on The National Archives' Discovery online catalogue **https://discovery.nationalarchives.gov.uk/**, using the keywords 'missing' or 'wanting'. You can narrow the search by using the reference for this census: HO 107.

There is a long list of the missing parishes on Findmypast (**https://www.findmypast.co.uk/articles/census-for-england-wales-and-scotland-missing-pieces**) and on Ancestry by each census (e.g. for 1851, see **https://www.ancestry.co.uk/search/collections/uki1851/**). The list includes parishes from the counties of Cheshire, Derbyshire, Hampshire, Kent, Middlesex, Northamptonshire, Oxfordshire, Somerset, Surrey, Wiltshire and Yorkshire.

There are countless examples of incorrect ages being given, though most are out by only a year or so, even allowing for enumerators rounding ages up or down to the nearest five. However, in the village of Peatling Parva, near Lutterworth in Leicestershire, two individuals gave their ages as 405 and 205.[6] Britons proved reluctant to reveal their true ages. The satirist George Cruikshank mocked the inaccuracy of ages in the collected census data, but his exaggeration may not have been far from the truth:

> … it appears that of the middle-aged population of these kingdoms, one in three has grown five years younger since the date of the last census; one in seven two years younger; one in twelve remains of the same age; one in thirty-eight is five years older than at the period referred to; and one in five hundred and sixty has attained the full age that might have been anticipated from the lapse of years.[7]

Householders should have been given written instructions telling them how to complete the form. Where householders were illiterate or confused by the new process, the enumerator helped to complete the schedule when he came to collect the form on the following day. In practice, many sets of instructions were not given out. Confusion thus remained as to how to fill out the schedules and whether to include lodgers and boarders.

Sadly, the 1841 census was recorded in pencil and parts have faded to illegibility. This caused great difficulty when family historians were restricted to searching on microfilm, but digital enhancement and zoom options on the commercial websites have now improved searches.

There are examples of householders who refused to appear on the census. Many remain unrecorded, but some were arrested and taken before their local magistrates' courts. The case of one Mr Clavering of London was recorded in the police intelligence column of *The Standard* of Saturday, 12 June 1841:[8]

MARLBOROUGH-STREET.– The Census.– Mr. Clavering, hosier, Regent's-quadrant, was summoned before Mr. Maltby for refusing to answer the questions of the enumerator appointed to take the census for that district.

Mr. Keith stated that he called on the defendant for the paper previously left, and at first was told that no paper had been received. When the paper was produced witness proceeded to put the inquiry sanctioned by Act of Parliament, whether the return was a true one; the defendant would not give an explicit answer, and when told that he was required, under a penalty, to give a proper reply, he – the Government for having legalised such as inquisitorial proceeding. Mr. Keith further added that, as the defendant was in respectable circumstances, he should beg the Court to inflict a high penalty. Mr. Keith further added that he had done no more than discharge a duty imposed upon him by the Legislature in putting the questions he did to the defendant.

Mr. Maltby said the defendant had rendered himself liable to the penalty of 5l. for his contumacious behaviour. The highest penalty, 5l., was then inflicted.

The defendant, with some warmth, told Mr. Keith he was d—d impertinent to put such questions to him.

Shortly after the defendant had quitted the Court a gentleman came in and begged Mr. Maltby to mitigate the penalty, on the grounds that Mr. Clavering was not in those flourishing circumstances that had been stated.

Mr. Maltby said looking at the defendant's refusal to answer the proper questions, in connection with the expressions which he had used, he did not feel inclined to alter his decision.

Other defences were more imaginative, such as that of the rector of Blaisdon, the Reverend William Black, who argued that God was against the census. In his defence he referred to the Bible, 2 Samuel, chapter 24, which he claimed proved that 'it is highly sinful to number the people.'[9]

How to Use the Census Effectively

As the results of this census can be inaccurate and unclear, it is important to be prepared when searching for a specific person. Be clear on the name variants your ancestors may have used. Middle names are rarely recorded on this census, but individuals may have used a second name or abbreviated form.

Ages are usually rounded up or down to the nearest five. Ensure that you use a broad age range in your web search.

Relationships are not recorded on this census, and it is important to beware of false presumptions. What appears to be a man and wife could be a brother and sister, for example. Take note of everyone in the household and all with the same surname. These details can be compared with other sources in order to establish identity and how the members of a household are related.

Occupants in one dwelling are separated from those in a neighbouring residence by a double forward slash '//'. A single '/' signifies the end of the entry for each family. However, there are many examples of enumerator error where the marks are in the wrong place, or extra marks were made in the CEBs later by clerks at the census office.

Where ancestors have a common name, they may be most easily identified by their occupation. However, people may have changed occupation in this period or have used a different job title. A joiner in the 1860s, for example, may appear as a carpenter, or even labourer, on the 1841 census. Where an occupant had more than one job, only the primary was to be noted. Women's occupations are poorly represented on this census (and sometimes later), with no acknowledgement of work in or from the home.

Taking it Further

As addresses are general and many persons were recorded away from home, contemporary records that show residence in this period are useful. For areas where rate books survive, these can help identify the rate-paying tenant and/or owner of a property. Old maps can provide further details on an area.

www.old-maps.co.uk/index.html and tithe records such as those of Cheshire (**https://maps.cheshireeast.gov.uk/tithemaps/**) or Norfolk (**http://www.historic-maps.norfolk.gov.uk/**) can help to locate your ancestors' home. For Scotland, the NLS has more than 48,000 zoomable map images online at **https://maps.nls.uk/**

To find out more about Chartist ancestors or political activity in the area your ancestors lived, the *Northern Star and Leeds General Advertiser* (1837–52), a Chartist newspaper, can be explored online at the free site, Nineteenth-century Serials Edition, **www.ncse.ac.uk**

Unique Features of the Non-English Censuses

The Scottish census is particularly valuable to family historians whose ancestors are not found in the baptism, marriage or burial records of the old parochial registers (OPRs). Civil registration would not be introduced in Scotland until 1855 and details on the census may be the only surviving record of a given ancestor. The census returns for Scottish shipping are held with those of the associated parish.

The 1841 census for Ireland largely no longer survives, with the exception of a few entries used for pension applications after 1908 and a handful of entries for parts of Galway and Cavan. Records of surviving parishes include the following:[10]

- Killeshandra, Cavan, except townlands of Corranea Glebe and Drumberry (NAI CEN 1841/1)
- Aglish, Kilkenny (*The Irish Ancestor*, 9 (1), pp.44–47, 1977)
- Rathkyran, Kilkenny (GO 683–4).

At NAI in Dublin, there are 1841 microfilm records for

- Cavan: Parish of Killeshandra
- Cork: fragments
- Waterford: fragments.

In Wales, the report revealed a high proportion of Welsh speakers: 'the population of Wales, by the census of 1841, was 1,045,753; of whom it was estimated that half a million either understand Welsh only or employ that language in their ordinary intercourse.'[11]

Summary

The 1841 census was the first modern census, and the first to be undertaken in the reign of Queen Victoria. It is also the first to be of specific use to family historians, mainly due to its introduction of individuals' names. The age and place of birth columns are less useful as many errors were made. The census caused confusion among the public and the enumerators. However, occupational details are helpful. This census followed less than four years after the introduction of civil registration in England and Wales and can be used by family historians to support details found in birth, marriage and death certificates. The census process itself underwent major changes, as did the personnel involved. From 1851, those overseeing the census would bring a more confident approach to population statistics, and a truly essential document for future family historians would be created.

Chapter 4

THE VICTORIAN CENSUS

Historical Context

KEY EVENTS OF 1841–1851

- 1842: Thomas Lister dies
- 1842: George Graham (1801–88) is appointed Registrar General
- 1844: William Donnelly (1805–79) is appointed Registrar General for Ireland
- 1846–52: Lord John Russell (Liberal) serves as prime minister
- 1845: Great Famine begins in Ireland
- 1847–48: Cholera epidemic
- 1848: Public Health Act.

In 1842, the first Registrar General and administrator of the 1841 census, Thomas Henry Lister, died in Westminster[1] of tuberculosis. His replacement was Major George Graham (1801–88), the brother of the then Home Secretary, Sir James Graham. The appointment was significant. In 1843, Sir James had tried to have a Factory Education Bill passed in Parliament. When this failed, Sir James blamed the general lack of statistics on public worship and school attendance in the UK. He felt that with recent data on religion and education, his bill could have been a success. It is perhaps no surprise, therefore, that when Sir James's brother designed the census of 1851, he introduced two extra sections asking for statistics on these very subjects.

Besides these, Major Graham oversaw notable changes in the taking and structure of the census. The mistakes of the previous census were learned and a new census Act was passed on 5 August 1850 (13 & 14 Vict., c. 53). The 1851 census would set the pattern for Victorian population administration from then on. One significant change was to move census night away from harvest time to the spring. In 1851, the census took place on Sunday, 30 March.

Previously the census had been supervised by a commissioner based at Somerset House. In 1851, the census was overseen by the statistician and epidemiologist, William Farr (1807–83), and his newly appointed assistant commissioner, Horace Mann (1823–1917). The new headquarters of census administration were in houses at Craigs Court, Charing Cross.[2] Farr and Mann were joined there by clerks from the Registrar General's department in Somerset House. Designer of the most significant developments of this census, Farr had joined the General Register Office in 1839 as compiler of abstracts. He used the position to become a world authority

William Farr (1807–1883).

on epidemiology, and his title was changed in recognition in 1842 to Superintendent of the Statistical Department. In 1851, he planned and wrote the main census report. The religious and education census reports were written by Horace Mann and published in 1854.

Since the last census, Ireland had been struck by tragedy. From September 1845, when the Irish potato crop had been struck by a devastating blight, hundreds of thousands of the population had fled famine for Britain and North America. The new assistant census commissioner of the Irish census, Dr William Wilde, worked on a survey that would reveal a marked increase in emigration.

Immigration from Ireland was of increasing concern in some parts of England and Scotland. In London, the Irish-born population increased by a third from 1841, up to 109,000.[3] Despite the problems caused in Ireland and to the working-class population in England, the upper-class politicians did little to ease the famine or reduce the number of deaths or migrants.

A short time after the census was taken, Charles Dickens' journal, *Household Words*, reported on the reduced Irish population:

The general results of the Census in Ireland are of a painful character. It appears that the present population is a little more than 6,500,000. The returns of the three preceding censuses were:– in 1841, 8,175,124; in 1831, 7,767,401; and in 1821, 6,801,827. So that the population of Ireland has diminished by a million and a half during the last ten years, and is not greater now than it was thirty years ago. It further appears that there is a great diminution in the number of houses as well as of inhabitants; that there is a decrease in the population of every county except Dublin; and that there is an increase in all the towns, amounting in Belfast to 32 per cent, and in Galway to no less than 43 per cent. The emigration from Great Britain and Ireland during the last ten years amounted to 1,494,786 persons; of whom it is estimated that nearly nine-tenths were Irish. And the population of England and Scotland has been increased by emigration from Ireland.[4]

The use of the census for medical statistics was increasingly popular among politicians, doctors and social administrators, both in Britain and Ireland. The census was used to measure deaths per 1,000 population. The resulting figure would serve as a barometer of the nation's health. This figure increased during the cholera epidemic, and in 1848 a Public Health Act was passed. This was designed to improve the living conditions of the rising numbers of urban poor and therefore to reduce death rates. A central Board of Health administered public health through local boards.

There were further changes to the administration of the census. In March 1851, *The Times* reported that 'A staff of 40,000 persons has been organized, who are to carry out the duty of distributing, collecting, examining, and digesting the printed forms issued by the Registrar General.'[5] This staff was broken down into 30,000 enumerators, acting under 2,190 registrars and 624 superintendent-registrars. Custom House and coastguard officers would enumerate merchant seamen and others on the waterways of Britain. Returns of the British army were to be sent to the Horse Guards, from where they would be forwarded to the census staff. All enumerators, sheriffs and schoolmasters were given forms by the census office.[6]

A new system of reporting occupations was also introduced. This grouped occupations into seventeen classes, plus a group for no stated occupation. The groups were as follows:[7]

Class 1:   Persons engaged in the Imperial or Local Government.
Class 2:   Persons engaged in the defence of the country.
Class 3:   Persons engaged in religion, law or medicine.
Class 4:   Persons engaged in art, literature, science and education.
Class 5:   Persons engaged in household duties, as wives, children, &c.
Class 6:   Persons engaged in boarding, lodging, domestic service and dress.
Class 7:   Persons engaged in commercial pursuits (merchants, bankers, &c.).

Class 8:   Persons engaged in conveyance.

Class 9:   Persons engaged in agriculture.

Class 10:   Persons engaged in breeding, animal tending and fishing.

Class 11:   Persons engaged in the higher branches of mechanical or chemical arts.

Class 12:   Workers or dealers in animal substances.

Class 13:   Workers and dealers in vegetable substances.

Class 14:   Mineral workers.

Class 15:   Unskilled or unspecified labour.

Class 16:   Persons of rank, property or independent means.

Class 17:   Useless or disabled members of society, criminals.

Within these classes were sub-classes. Unlike in 1841, when only one occupation could be recorded, this time individuals 'following more than one distinct trade may insert his occupations in the order of importance'.

Women's employment was also better recorded in 1851: women 'employed from home, or at home, in any but domestic duties, are to be distinctly recorded'. This included the many female milliners, laundresses and others of the working classes.

The schedule across the UK was extended to include exact place of birth, although many people continued to enter only the county or country rather than the town, city or parish. The reports would arrange population tables around the newer registration counties, districts, sub-districts, parishes and townships. This was a move away from the 1841 practice of using older units, such as hundreds, wapentakes, sokes, liberties and parishes.[8] In 1851, the enumerators' returns noted the parish or township, ecclesiastical district, city or borough, town and/or village.

The census was recorded in pen and ink from this date on, although some enumerators continued to use pencils. However, there remained problems associated with how the papers were stored, and many have been lost or damaged over the years.

Although a relationship column was introduced, care should be taken over the terms son-in-law and daughter-in-law, which in the past could be used to mean stepson and stepdaughter as we understand them today.

What Details are Included?

The registrars gave the following documents to the enumerators:

- Householders' schedules
- Enumeration books
- Forms for places of worship, schools and literary institutions

- Instructions to enumerators
- Books for public institutions – for institutions (i.e. workhouses, prisons, lunatic asylums and barracks) which the Registrar General selected for separate enumeration
- List of places of worship, schools and literary associations.

As with the 1841 census, the enumerators handed out the enumeration forms to households in the week leading up to the census night and they collected the forms on the Monday. The information given on the forms was written up into enumerators' books. As with the 1841 schedules, the household schedules for 1851 were destroyed. The books were sent to Census House, where they were reviewed by the clerks of the General Register Office.

The census enumerators' books requested the following:[9]

Page i: Description of enumeration district with geographical data.

Page ii: Summary table of the total number of houses, occupiers and persons in each of the pages for nominal information.

Page iii: Summary tables for the number of itinerants and the temporary increase and decrease of the population.

Page iv: Declarations signed by the enumerator, registrar and superintendent registrar.

Page v: Directions for filling up the book.

Pages vi–vii: Example of how to fill up the book.

Pages 1–x: Pages for inserting nominal information.

In 1854, these books were sent to the Public Record Office. The returns were only deposited there in 1912.

The headings on the household schedules are as follows:

- NUMBER OF SCHEDULE
- NAME OF STREET, PLACE OR ROAD AND NAME OR NUMBER OF HOUSE
- NAME AND SURNAME OF EACH PERSON WHO ABODE IN THE HOUSE, ON THE NIGHT OF THE 30TH MARCH, 1851
- RELATION TO HEAD OF FAMILY
- CONDITION
- AGE OF Males
  Females

- RANK, PROFESSION, OR OCCUPATION
- WHERE BORN
- WHETHER BLIND OR DEAF-AND-DUMB.

The summary tables in the enumerators' books asked for the following:

- Number of separate occupiers, houses (inhabited, uninhabited, being built), males and females recorded on each page of the nominal returns
- As in first table but for each named parish or township. Persons to be divided into those in and out of houses
- Estimated number of males and females in vessels on inland navigable waters, in barns or sheds, in tents and in the open air
- Number of males and females temporarily present
- Number of males and females temporarily absent.

The first name was to be written in full, but enumerators were advised to use only initials or first letters for any middle names.

For this census, a new classification system for occupations was introduced. This system required that masters in trade and manufacture include 'master' in their occupation details. Master farmers had to include the number of acres they occupied and the number of labourers in their employ.

Religious Census

The religious census formed a separate clause of the census, although it was held on the same day. Each church or chapel, of whichever religious persuasion, was asked:

I   Name and Description of Church or Chapel
II   Where situated
III   When opened for Worship
IV   How or by whom erected; Cost, how defrayed
V   Stipend of Minister
VI   Free Sittings
VII   Estimated Number of Attendants on March 30, 1851; Average number of attendants in preceding months
VIII Remarks
IX   Signature, &c.

Returns were variable because they relied on the willingness of clergy or church wardens, not only to complete the returns but also to estimate and eliminate double and treble counting of those who attended a service more than once on that day.

Assistant Commissioner Horace Mann's report on religious worship in England and Wales was published in January 1854. The results shocked Victorian society. In what was considered to be a Christian nation, it was estimated that only 7,261,032 out of a total population of 17,927,609 had attended a service at church or chapel. Allowing for those who could not attend because of illness or other duties, the total number of absentees was 5,288,294. The figure was all the more surprising as the census had been taken on Mothering Sunday, when a higher-than-normal attendance might have been expected.

The results also showed that the Church of England was not as dominant as it would have wished. This was an embarrassment for what was the national church of England, Wales and Ireland at the time; only 52 per cent of those attending a service went to Church of England services. Although a slight majority, it was a figure that embarrassed Anglicans and delighted Nonconformists. With the restoration of the Roman Catholic episcopacy the previous year – known at the time as the Papal Aggression – the established church found itself under acute pressure.

Although the religious census does not provide records of individuals, and records of individual churches have not survived, it is an invaluable reminder of the character of the peoples of the British Isles in the middle of the nineteenth century.[10] The report also revealed that church attendance was less in towns than in rural areas. The Scottish religious census, unlike that of England and Wales, has not survived. All that remains are the report, which can be read on HISTPOP, and parts that survive in local or private collections. Genealogist Chris Paton found two completed census forms among the kirk sessions papers for Speymouth and Garmouth Preaching Station in Morayshire (National Records of Scotland (NRS) ref. CH2/839/20).[11] Among other details, it reveals that of the 3,116 Scottish congregations to make the 1851 religious census, only 904 were Church of Scotland. A similar exercise was never attempted again, although the *British Weekly* newspaper conducted a religious census in London in 1886 (published as *The Religious Census of London* by Hodder and Stoughton in 1888) and the *Daily News* did likewise in 1902/3 (published by Hodder and Stoughton in 1904 as *The Religious Life of London*).[12]

Education Census

The education census involved enumerators asking each householder if a school took place in his or her house. At each house where teaching occurred, the enumerator would then leave an education census schedule for them to complete in addition to that of the household. The schedules asked for the following details:

- religious and secular affiliation
- date of establishment
- income and expenditure
- number of teachers (their sex, pay and levels of training)
- number of pupils (their age, sex and number attending on census day)
- subjects of instructions (number of pupils being instructed)
- classroom sizes
- occupations of evening scholars
- appointment of school governors.

Few schedules survive from the education census. Those that do are held at The National Archives in reference series HO 129 among the returns of the ecclesiastical census. Parts of this series of records can be downloaded for free as part of TNA's Digital Microfilms project via the Discovery portal **http://discovery.nationalarchives.gov.uk**

Finding Aids

Finding aids are similar to those for the 1841 census records. As with that census, indexes exist on the major commercial website providers (see below).

The National Archives' series code for this census is HO 107, the same as for the 1841 census. This is the only occasion on which the code is repeated. The subsequent censuses would each be given a unique code. As noted above, the ecclesiastical census and remaining parts of the education census are archived in HO 129.

Indexes have also been produced by a number of family history societies. Some of these are available via their respective websites. Others are in book form.

Online Resources

The 1851 census indexes, transcriptions and images for England, Wales, the Channel Islands and the Isle of Man are included on Ancestry, MyHeritage, UK Census Online, TheGenealogist, Genes Reunited, Findmypast and RootsUK. FamilySearch offers free access to an index and transcriptions for this year, with a link to view images at the commercial Findmypast website. Free data is also available at FreeCEN, CensusFinder and Genuki.

Findmypast includes address, occupation, other household members and census reference search options. MyHeritage includes residence, other household members and keyword search options.

Indexes and brief transcriptions for the Scottish 1851 census can be viewed on Ancestry, Genes Reunited and Findmypast. MyHeritage has a census extract for a small percentage of this. The only website to give full access to the images of the Scottish censuses is ScotlandsPeople.

Free Resources

Currently the FreeCen website of UK census transcriptions (**www. freecen.org.uk**) provides free access to the 1851 census data for some parishes in the following counties:

Aberdeenshire	Fife	Perthshire
Angus	Gloucestershire	Renfrewshire
Argyllshire	Hertfordshire	Ross & Cromarty
Ayrshire	Inverness-shire	Roxburghshire
Banffshire	Kincardineshire	Selkirkshire
Bute	Kinross-shire	Somerset
Caithness	Lanarkshire	Stirlingshire
Clackmannanshire	Midlothian	Sussex
Cornwall	Morayshire	Sutherland
Devon	Nairnshire	Wigtownshire
Dunbartonshire	Orkney	Wiltshire
East Lothian	Peeblesshire	

Census transcriptions for parishes in Dumfriesshire, Kirkcudbrightshire and Wigtownshire have been digitized by the Friends of the Archives of Dumfries and Galloway at **https://info.dumgal.gov.uk/ HistoricalIndexes**

The name and street indexes to the water-damaged 1851 census returns can be explored at **www.1851-unfilmed.org.uk**. The original images are available to view on Ancestry.

As with the 1841 census, many of the online parish clerk (OPC) websites for specific counties give transcriptions of the 1851 census for certain parishes in their locality; for example, the parish of Bunny in Nottinghamshire **http://www.bunnyvillage.org.uk/cen1851.htm**. A full list of these is in the Appendices. Other free local census databases can be found through Family History Societies Online, **www.fhs-online.co.uk/ databases.php**

Problems

Many clergymen were unhappy with the separate schedules they were required to complete, particularly the questions about their financial position. However, they could complete this at their discretion. There was also disquiet about the demands of the schoolmasters' schedules.

Again, as in 1841, not all in the population were enumerated. A Cornelius Carter of 29 Grosvenor Street, Grosvenor Square wrote to *The Times*, complaining that:

> No Census paper was left at this house, nor has there been any inquiry made since relative thereto.
>
> Now, if such neglect can be shown in so prominent a situation, how much more likely is it to have happened in poorer and more densely crowded neighbourhoods, and how much faith is to be placed in the accuracy of the returns?[13]

In response, the registrar of the district (of Grosvenor Square) replied:

> ... the house in question is a corner one having a separate entrance in two streets for each of which streets there was a distinct enumerator; that the enumerator in whose district it was arranged to include it being taken ill, a substitute had to be found, who, although called upon to act on the shortest notice, and without time to receive minute instructions, did call at the house, and was there informed that it was not to be included in the street for which he enumerated.[14]

Although the registrar seemed to regard this case as 'exceptional', there are further examples of missing persons.

Seamen and members of the Royal Navy were enumerated in this census, but they were administered separately and many of their records have not survived. No separate census of the British army was undertaken in this year. However, military genealogist Kevin Asplin has compiled the 1851 Worldwide Army Index from musters contained in WO 10/11-12 Series War Office Paylists held at The National Archives, Kew. The index lists all officers and other ranks subjects serving with British and colonial regiments in the January-March quarter of 1851 together with their regimental HQ location. The index is effectively a military surrogate for the 1851 census taken on 30 March 1851. Among the almost 250,000 included are recruits, boy soldiers, bandsmen and civilians working in the armed forces as clerks, pension recruiters and suchlike. Additional notes feature detachments, attachments, and units recruits would likely join. The 1851 Worldwide Army Index can be searched on the Forces War Records database, TheGenealogist and Findmypast.

Findmypast has a list of missing census material at **https://www. findmypast.co.uk/articles/census-for-england-wales-and-scotland-missing-pieces**. Ancestry has a list of missing parts of the 1851 English census at **https://www.ancestry.co.uk/search/collections/uki1851/**. The missing parts can also be identified through The National Archives' Discovery engine **https://discovery.nationalarchives.gov.uk** using the keywords 'missing' or 'wanting', and restricting the search to reference HO 107.

One part of this census that was damaged was for the area of Manchester, then in the county of Lancashire. For the most part, the records have since been found again and images for the areas of Manchester, Chorlton, Salford, Oldham and Ashton-under-Lyne can be seen on the Ancestry and Findmypast websites. Ancestry has also digitized scans of the damaged parts (see image). Some of these show more detail than others. This example, of a street in Salford, has suffered major damage. The data for Blackley, Harpurhey and Moston were missing, along with parts of

Screenshot showing a scan of Ancestry of the damaged 1851 Manchester census (Salford District 1a).

Hulme, St George's and London Road districts. Many of the records for Deansgate, Ardwick and Chorlton-on-Medlock are illegible.

The Manchester & Lancashire Family History Society transcribed surviving sections and these were published on microfiche and on CD-ROM at the Manchester Room at City Library. A name index is available at a dedicated website **www.1851-unfilmed.org.uk** for the damaged material and this material is now available on their website. Some entries which are not found in the Ancestry transcriptions can be found on Findmypast.

Although individuals who were away from home on census night should have been enumerated at the place they were then, many were confused by the instructions. This can lead to some people not being recorded and others being recorded twice. The latter was common with small children who spent the night with a relative: they would be recorded there and at their parents' home.

How to Use the Census Effectively

On this census the residence details are given more fully. From this, the exact address can be plotted on a contemporary map. Local record offices should hold good collections of historical maps. Reprints of old Ordnance Survey maps have been reproduced by Alan Godfrey and are available via **www.alangodfreymaps.co.uk**. The 1851 address can also be compared with the abode of the same family in 1841. This could show that the address is the same, or that the household has moved. Using these alongside addresses given on parish or civil registration records should clarify this.

For the first time, householders were asked to acknowledge family members with various disabilities. However, there is only one column for this and very little space for recording the disability. There may be marks in this column that are simply mistakes. For confirmation of disability, the relevant individual should be identified on further censuses. Death certificates and hospital or asylum records can also be useful.

Another column indicated the relationship to the head of the household. This is particularly useful when trying to separate a wife, sister or daughter of the same name. Marital status ('condition') is also noted, and may help to identify a deceased relative where the spouse is described as a 'widow'. Again, it is useful to compare the details here with those of the 1841 census. When all surviving members of a household in 1841 are identified in 1851, their relationships with each other should be clear.

Taking it Further

The most controversial part of this census was the clause concerning places of worship, as explored above. Unlike previous censuses, when inhabitants had been asked to give details of numbers of baptisms, marriages and burials, they were asked for information

respecting all Churches and Chapels, and Places of Public Religious Worship, in order that it may be ascertained how far the means of Religious Instruction provided in Great Britain during the last fifty years has kept pace with the population during the same period, and to what extent those means are adequate to meet the spiritual wants of the increased population of 1851; also respecting all Schools, in order that it may be ascertained what means of instruction are within the reach of the various classes of the community.[15]

1851 Census of Llanwrin, Montgomeryshire. (© Crown Copyright Images reproduced by courtesy of The National Archives, London, England. *www.NationalArchives.gov.uk* & *www.TheGenealogist.co.uk*)

George Graham did emphasize that 'There is no legal obligation upon you to respond to the various inquiries', and many did not.

In Wales, the census revealed that roughly 80 per cent of religious adherents were Nonconformists, whereas only an approximate 20 per cent attended the Church of England. Welsh families, like the Jones family in this image (1851 Llanwrin ref. HO107/2495/, p.216), were thus more likely to be found in Nonconformist records. Even though this census entry gives the younger Jones children's birthplace as Llanwrin, none have been found in the parish baptism records. A similar problem exists for Scotland. ScotlandsPeople includes baptism records for Church of Scotland and Roman Catholics only, neglecting those who attended the 2,018 other Nonconformist religious institutions noted in the census.

This was the first census that assessed the marital status of the population.

The number of females in the population was noticeably higher than that of males: 10,743,747 in contrast with 10,192,721. There was some concern that there were too many unmarried women.

Llanwrin Parish Church.

Local 1851 censuses exist at the respective English local record offices of Goodnestone in Kent, Bilney and Beetley in Norfolk, Kinoulton, Farndon and Balderton in Nottinghamshire, Standlake in Oxfordshire, Aston-by-Stone in Staffordshire, Ewhurst in Surrey, and Graffham and Woolavington in Sussex.

The population of Great Britain had grown from the time of the 1841 census to 21,104,072, of which 167,604 were out of the country serving in the army, navy or on merchant vessels. The urban population had grown even further, with 6.3 million people now living in cities of 20,000 or more.

In 1851, Henry Mayhew's journalistic articles on *London Labour and the London Poor* (G. Woodfall & Son, 1851) were published in three volumes under this title. This work gives great insight into working lives of the capital, and will be of particular interest if your ancestor was one of the thousands of London poor in the 1840s or in 1851. Mayhew makes several references to the census, comparing what he sees around him with the statistics of the 1841 report:

> I am told by a London hawker of soft goods, or packman, that a number of his craft, hawking London and its vicinity as far as he can judge, is about 120 (the census of 1841 makes the London hawkers, hucksters and pedlars amount to 2,041). In the 120 are included the Irish linen hawkers. I am also informed that the fair trader's profits amount to about 20 per cent, while those of the not over-particular trader range from 80 to 200 per cent. In a fair way of business it is said the hawker's taking will amount, upon an average, to 7l. or 8l. per week; whereas the receipts of the 'duffer', or unfair hawker, will sometimes reach to 50l. per week. Many, however, travel days, and do not turn a penny.

Horace Mann's report on school provision and attendance was published in March 1854. The report concluded that most children in England and Wales received some form of schooling. However, critics have argued that this was optimistic.

Unique Features of the Non-English Censuses

The Scottish census for this year was written in brown ink on blue paper, which can affect legibility online. Once again, the Scottish census provided a record of some people who were unrecorded in the OPRs. If you have ancestors who died between June 1841 and the introduction of civil registration in Scotland in 1855, the census return may be the only record of them. If their baptisms were not recorded in the OPRs, the birthplace column on this census could help you to confirm where they were from. Unlike the 1841 census, this should reveal the parish and county of birth.

In Wales, at their request, some households were given schedules written in Welsh.

The census of Ireland for 1851 was undertaken by William Donnelly, the Registrar General, who acted as chief commissioner. Edward Singleton was secretary. Most enumerators were drawn from the police, as they had been in 1841.

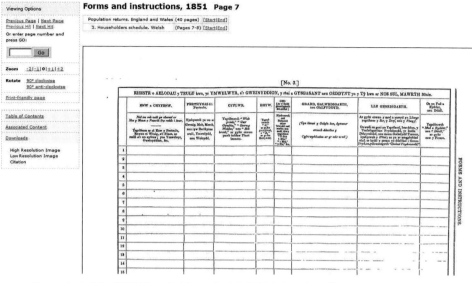

Screenshot of the 1851 Householders schedule Welsh from http://histpop.org.

The schedule asked for the following:

- Name
- Age
- Sex
- Relationship to head of the family
- Marital status
- Year of marriage
- Occupation
- Education (either 'Read', 'Read and Write' or 'Cannot Read')
- Irish language
- Place of birth
- Whether deaf, dumb or blind.

A second schedule asked for details of family members who were absent on census night.

A third schedule sought details of those who had died in the previous ten years.

Other forms dealt with institutions and ships:

Form A: Family return (the main form distributed to all households)
Form B: Ship return
Form C: Families where members were sick on census night

Form D: Separate return of the insane and idiots
Form E1: Workhouse return
Form E2: Workhouse return (sickness)
Form E3: Workhouse return (deaths in past ten years)
Form F: Hospital return (two tables: ordinary and deaths)
Form G: College/boarding school return
Form H: Barrack return
Form I: Asylum/gaol return (two tables: ordinary and deaths)
Form K: Prison/Bridewell return
Form L: School attendance return
Form O: Emigrant/passenger return
Form P: Inquest return

Parliamentary Papers for the census of Ireland are arranged by county and can be accessed at the HISTPOP website. The statistics for the area, population and number of houses of the County of Carlow, for example, can be read at **http://histpop.org/ohpr/servlet**

The nationally held collection of the 1851 census of Ireland was destroyed. However, a few local collections remain. These include the following 1851 census records, which have been microfilmed and can be viewed at the NAI:

Antrim	13 parishes	Aghagallon, Aghalee, Aghoghil, Ballinderry, Ballymoney, Carncastle, Dunaghy, Grange of Killyglen, Killead, Kilwaughter, Larne, Rasharkin, Tickmacrevan
Cork	5 parishes	Kilcrumper, Kilworth, Leitrim, Macrony, Kilworth
Dublin City	22 parishes	Heads of household and streets only

In addition, all Presbyterians recorded in the 1851 census of Loughinisland, County Down are named in the *Family Links* journal, 1 (6), September 1982, pp.5–11, and 1 (7), January 1983, pp.9–14. Names of those in Scarva, County Down can be found at the Representative Church Body Library in Dublin (ref. Ms. 65).

The 1851 census of Clonee townland in Drumkeeran, County Fermanagh is held at the NAI in reference CEN 1851/13/1.

The 1851 census of Aglish, County Kilkenny is published in the *Irish Ancestor*, 9 (2), 1977, pp.129–33. The censuses of Portnascully and Rathkyran are held at the Genealogical Office, Dublin in reference 683–4.

All Church of Ireland members of Clogherny in County Tyrone are named with ages in the PRONI, ref. D10 4/32C/9/4/2, 5 and T877 (839).

Full reports on the Irish census can be found at HISTPOP.

The 1851 census abstracts for Ireland are available on Ancestry. These records were created by genealogist Josephine Masterson from information that appeared on the 1841 and 1851 Irish censuses. Masterson used old-age pension records (dating from 1908) where the elderly applicants proved their ages by submitting facts that were checked against entries in the 1841 and 1851 census records. The original details had been recorded in summary books before the census was destroyed by fire. Masterson also used available census fragments, certified copies of portions of some returns, family transcriptions and other records. More transcriptions for Irish censuses in this year can be found at **www.searchforancestors.com/locality/ireland/census1851** and **www.ulsterancestry.com/ua-free-pages.php**.

A CD-ROM containing 60,000 names and addresses of heads of households of Dublin, which were transcribed before the census data was destroyed, is available from Eneclann (**www.eneclann.ie**).

Summary

Often referred to as the 'Victorian census', the count of 1851 introduced a system and personnel that would take the process forward successfully through many decades. This was the first census overseen by Major George Graham and Dr William Farr, and both men took a confident approach to census-taking and population statistics. The 1851 census was most memorable for its education census and the controversial religious census. The revelations of this event would affect social and political opinion and colour the approach to the next census of 1861.

Chapter 5

1861: THE FIRST SEPARATE SCOTTISH CENSUS

Historical Context

KEY EVENTS OF 1851–1861

- 1854: William Pitt Dundas (1801–83) is appointed first Registrar General of Scotland
- 1854: Cholera epidemic
- 1853–56: Crimean War
- 1855: Civil registration is introduced in Scotland
- 1855–8: Henry John Temple, Lord Palmerston (1784–1865) serves as prime minister
- 1857: Matrimonial Causes Act moves jurisdiction over divorce from ecclesiastical to civil courts, thereby enabling more Britons to obtain a divorce
- 1857: Indian Mutiny
- 1861: Death of Prince Albert
- 1859–65: Lord Palmerston serves as prime minister for the second time.

In 1861, the GRO, still headed by George Graham, the Registrar General, approached the Home Office to call for an Act for the creation of the census. This Act, 23 & 24 Vict., c. 61, was passed by Parliament on 6 August 1860. Dr William Farr was once again a commissioner for the census.

By this time, the Victorian Age was well established. Queen Victoria had settled into her role as monarch and was happily married to Prince Albert, by whom she now had nine children. Britain was a confident industrial nation, with a major international position. The census of 1861 reflects this, revealing an increase in the number of industrial workers and the growth of urban areas compared with ten years earlier.

Following the Indian Mutiny of 1857, the British government had taken more direct control of the Indian subcontinent from the East India Company and consolidated its position as a major imperial power. Britain led the world in manufacturing, although few industrial innovations had taken place in recent years. This strong economic position was attended by increased wealth, but constant industrial growth had created unhealthy and often dangerous living conditions in overcrowded urban areas. The working classes were at risk of death or serious injury in the factories, workshops or mines where they toiled.

This was a situation that concerned authors such as Charles Dickens, and industrialists and philanthropists like Titus Salt. The northern textile manufacturer had recently created a model village for his employees near Bradford in West Yorkshire. This village was christened Saltaire, and included houses, bathhouses, an educational institute, a hospital, almshouses and a Congregational church. The statistics provided by the censuses would help provide supporting evidence for the reports and articles of Dickens, Salt and others who demanded social change in this period.

During the 1854 National Education (Ireland) debate, the Earl of Clancarty, arguing that the school system should be improved, referred to the census abstract of the county of Clare, 'where the national system is in full operation – that in the course of the decennial period, from 1841 to 1851 ignorance had decreased only in the ratio of one per cent of the population, and that in the civic districts ignorance had actually increased to the extent of ten per cent.'[1] The census had contributed to change in other areas, too. Evidence from the 1841 census showing women and children employed in mines influenced the Mines Act of the following year. Lord Shaftesbury's 1842 Act banned the employment underground of all females and males under the age of 10.

The cholera outbreak of 1854, one of many in the first half of Victoria's reign, proved to Farr and his colleagues that Britain needed the medical statistics he so highly prized. Although with increasing prosperity, births in the succeeding years exceeded deaths, the demand for labour in the expanding factories and mines meant that the number of deaths from infectious disease, accidents and other causes remained high. The Crimean War of 1853–56 – in which more men died of disease than from battle – highlighted the lack of hygiene and medical care in the British army. The work of Florence Nightingale and Mary Seacole during the war and the consequent establishment of a trained and organized nursing force helped to transform hospitals and contributed to improved public health.

Culturally, the urban working classes were creating a new identity. Many turned to Methodism, attracted by its values of equality and the promise of reward for hard work. Education and self-development were also popular, with a growth in the number of evening classes and working men's colleges. Through these institutions, the working classes came together to discuss social and political ideas. During this time, the foundations of the trade union movement were laid.

All did not run smoothly for Palmerston in the preparation for the census. A suggestion was made that, as in Ireland, each occupier should state his or her religious profession. This was to challenge the conclusion of the 1851 census that there were almost as many Dissenters in England and Wales as there were members of the established church. Palmerston was visited by a deputation from the Conservatives, led by Benjamin Disraeli, to whom he gave his assurance that the religious clause would remain. Nevertheless, complaints came from councils and religious leaders across the country. By June, Palmerston was lobbied by members of his own (Liberal) party who requested he withdraw the clause. Eventually, pressure against the religious census won and only in Ireland was a count taken of religious adherence. Palmerston and his Home Secretary were also lobbied by the Committee of the Social Science Association of London, headed by the philanthropist, Lord Shaftesbury. This committee argued for inclusion in the census of the number of rooms in houses and the number of children attending schools.[2]

As in 1851, the enumerators distributed schedules to householders in the week leading up to the census night. The heads of each household were to complete these, if able, and the 30,441 enumerators in England and Wales would collect the next day – Monday, 8 April – setting out at sunrise. On the following page is a screenshot from HISTPOP that shows an original schedule for the 'Islands in the British Seas' (i.e. the Isle of Man, Alderney, Guernsey and Jersey). This is similar to the layout in the census enumerators' books, but includes a space for a signature in the bottom right-hand corner. The completed schedules were sent to the census office and have since been destroyed.

The enumerators' returns were organized by parish (or township), city or municipal borough, municipal ward, parliamentary borough, town, hamlet or tithing, and ecclesiastical district. The town was noted where the area was not a city or a borough. England and Wales were divided into 635 registration districts. For this year, enumerators had to note in each dwelling the number of rooms that had windows. Householders

1861 Schedule on the HISTPOP website.

were instructed to complete the returns correctly, or else face a fine of a maximum £5.

In Scotland, where civil registration had been introduced in 1855, the separate General Register Office for Scotland (GROS) in Edinburgh was established eighteen years after the GRO in England and Wales. In 1854, William Pitt Dundas was appointed as the first Registrar General for Scotland. This development was significant for the taking of the census from that time onwards. While the census had been administered previously from London, with similar questions being asked, from 1861 the Scottish census was administered separately. Pitt Dundas was assisted in the task by the Superintendent of Statistics. Twelve staff were recruited to the statistical branch of the GROS, but more were needed in order to complete the census work. This took three years, eventually being completed on 10 February 1864.

In Ireland, the census was overseen by the Registrar General and chief commissioner, William Donnelly, and his assistant commissioners, William R. Wilde and George W. Abraham. They were based at the census office in Henrietta Street, Dublin. Instead of enumerators, the police and others collected the census details in writing.

What Details are Included?
In 1861, official crew lists and naval schedules were taken, many of which do survive. These can be used to find the location of the vessels. This census included those serving on Royal Navy (RN) ships overseas. For example, Commander Walter Strickland, who was living in Malta,

was recorded as a visitor on board the *Victor Emanuel*, which was serving in the Mediterranean.

In England, Wales and Islands in the British Seas, household schedules asked the following:

- NAME AND SURNAME
  No Person ABSENT on the Night of Sunday, April 7th, to be entered here; EXCEPT those who may be TRAVELLING or out at WORK during that Night, and who RETURN HOME ON MONDAY, April 8th.– Write after the Name of the Head of the Family the names of his Wife, Children, and other Relatives: then Visitors, &c., and Servants.
- RELATION TO HEAD OF FAMILY
  State whether Wife, Son, Daughter, or other Relative, Visitor, Boarder, &c., or Servant.
- CONDITION
  Write either 'Married', 'Widower', 'Widow', or 'Unmarried', against the Names of all Persons except Young Children.
- SEX
  Write 'M' against Males and 'F' against Females.
- AGE (LAST BIRTHDAY)
  For Infants under One Year state the Age in Months, writing 'Under 1 Month', '1 Month', '2 Months', &c.
- RANK, PROFESSION, OR OCCUPATION
  (Before filling up this Column, you are requested to read the Instructions on the other side.)
- WHERE BORN
  Opposite the Names of those born in England, write the County, and Town or Parish. If born in Scotland, Ireland, the British Colonies or the East Indies, state the Country. If born in Foreign parts state the Country; and if also a British Subject add 'British Subject' or 'Naturalised British Subject', as the case may be.
- IF DEAF-AND-DUMB, OR BLIND
  Write 'Deaf-and-Dumb', or 'Blind', opposite the Name of the Person; and if so from Birth, add 'from Birth'.

A separate crew list was designed of 'the Officers, Crew, and Marines, as well as Passengers and Visitors, on Board Her Majesty's Ship – on the Night of Sunday, April 7th, 1861.'

- NAME AND SURNAME
  Write, after the Name of the Captain, the Names of the other Officers, of the Petty Officers, of the Seamen, of Marines, and of Boys; the Names of Passengers and Visitors on Board are to follow.

- RANK OR QUALITY
  If not belonging to the Ship, state whether a Passenger (P); or, a Visitor (V).
- CONDITION
  Whether 'Single', 'Married', 'Widower', or 'Widow'.
- AGE OF Males
  Females
- WHERE BORN
  Opposite the Names of those born in England, Scotland, or Ireland, write the County, and Town or Period. If here in the British Colonies, or the East Indies, state the Colony, &c. If born in Foreign parts state the Country; or if also a British Subject add 'British Subject', or 'Naturalised British Subject', as the case may be.

The census enumerators' books included summary tables of the following:

- Number of males and females temporarily absent, and the reasons for their absence
- Number of males and females temporarily present, and the reasons for their presence
- Number of schedules, houses (inhabited, uninhabited, being built), males and females in each named parish or township, or parts thereof. Persons to be divided into those in and out of houses
- Number of above on each page of the nominal returns.

1861 example of a census enumerator's book on the HISTPOP website.

This image from HISTPOP shows the summary table on page 4 of a census enumerator's book for 1861. This enumerator was working in district 23, Aston, Warwickshire.

The reports for each registration district of 1861 included:[3]

- The ages of males and females in five-year age groups
- The number of children (males and females) under five
- The civil (marital) condition of males and females broken down by age group
- The occupations of males aged 20 and over
- The occupations of females aged 20 and over
- The birthplaces of males and females aged under 20, and 20 and over
- The numbers of blind, deaf and dumb people
- The inmates of workhouses, prisons, lunatic asylums and hospitals.

Registrars were required to forward copies of vital events and a table was compiled of causes of death in England and Wales. The authorities in the 'Islands in the British Seas' did not have to forward these documents.

The population of England, Wales and the Islands in the British Seas according to the 1861 census was 20,205,504: an increase of more than 2 million people over the decade and double the number – 10,087,768 – in 1811.

In Scotland, the schedule requested the following:

THE UNDERMENTIONED HOUSES ARE SITUATE WITHIN THE BOUNDARIES OF THE PARISH OF/QUOAD SACRA PARISH OF/PARLIAMENTARY BURGH OF/ROYAL BURGH OF/TOWN OF/ VILLAGE OF

- No. of Schedule
- Road, Street, &c., and No. or Name of House
- Houses
  Inhabited
  Uninhabited (U), or Building (B)
- Name and Surname of each Person
- Relation to Head of Family
- Condition
- Age of
  Males
  Females
- Rank, Profession, or Occupation
- Where Born

- Whether Blind, or Deaf and Dumb
- Number of Children from 5 to 13 attending School or being educated at Home
- Rooms with One or more Windows.

Finding Aids

Surname, place and street indexes are available at The National Archives. Other indexes have been published by family history societies, such as the *1861 Census Index Horsforth* (Wharfedale Family History Group, 1998) and several parishes in the Lothian area published by the Lothian FHS (see **www.lothianfhs.org**).

Detailed census indexes are available on each of the major commercial genealogy website providers.

Street indexes are held at The National Archives and relevant local record offices. The National Archives' code for this census is RG 9.

Online Resources

Online records and search devices of the 1861 census are similar to those of 1851.

TheGenealogist, Ancestry and Findmypast allow separate searches of the crew lists for this census. On Findmypast, they can be seen by clicking on 'Ships and Overseas establishments' in the 'County' section. Ancestry allows users to 'Browse collection' and then select 'Royal Navy' from the 'County' section. From there a drop-down box appears with the names of ships. MyHeritage has a keyword search option.

A worldwide army (or soldier) index has been compiled from pay lists of the Royal Artillery, Royal Engineers and the cavalry, guards, infantry and other units, which are held at The National Archives in series WO 10, WO 11 and WO 12. It includes men serving overseas. The index is believed to name around 98 per cent of 'other ranks' serving in the British army in 1861. The index can be searched on Findmypast.

A specific site for the 1861 census, linked to TheGenealogist website, can be searched at **www.uk1861census.com/census_online.htm**.

Free Resources

The FreeCen website provides links to transcriptions of census data for some parishes in the following counties:

Anglesey	Bedfordshire	Caernarvonshire
Argyllshire	Berkshire	Caithness
Banffshire	Bute	Cambridgeshire

Channel Islands	Huntingdonshire	Renfrewshire
Cornwall	Isle of Man	Roxburghshire
Cumberland	Kent	Rutland
Denbighshire	Kinross-shire	Scottish shipping
Devon	Lancashire	Selkirkshire
Dorset	Leicestershire	Shropshire
Dumfriesshire	Lincolnshire	Somerset
County Durham	Middlesex	Staffordshire
East Lothian	Morayshire	Sussex
East Riding of	Nairnshire	Warwickshire
Yorkshire	Norfolk	Westmoreland
England and Wales	Northumberland	Wigtownshire
Shipping	North Riding of	Wiltshire
Flintshire	Yorkshire	Worcestershire
Gloucestershire	Nottinghamshire	West Riding of
Hampshire	Peeblesshire	Yorkshire

FamilySearch provides free access to a detailed index of the 1861 English and Welsh census, as well as an option to browse images. Images connected to index results can be viewed via Findmypast or at a Family History Centre. The Sheffield census addendum can be searched online at **http://www.baseportal.com/cgi-bin/baseportal.pl?htx=/sheffielddfhs2/full_search2**. This is connected to the work of the Sheffield Indexers at **www.sheffieldIndexers.com**.

Problems

Around 3 per cent of the 1861 census returns are known to be missing or damaged.

In London, the missing or damaged sections have been identified.[4] These include the census returns for Pimlico, Belgravia sub-district, parts of Westminster and part of Woolwich Arsenal.

Of registration districts in the City, the following are missing:

- part of the parish of St Dunstan in the West (RG9/219)
- parts of Cliffords Inn and Serjeants Inn within that parish (RG9/221)
- part of the parish of St Gregory by St Paul (RG9/220)
- the first six pages of the parish of St Bride (RG9/221)
- part of the Inner Temple (RG9/221); part of the parish of St Mary Staining (RG9/222)
- part of the parish of St Michael-le-Quern (RG9/223)
- part of St Botolph-without-Bishopsgate
- Houndsditch (RG9/212, folios 140–3).

Chelsea district is only 92.5 per cent complete, with the three sub-districts missing different proportions:

- Sub-district 1 Chelsea South (RG9 30–32)
- Sub-district 2 Chelsea North West (RG9 33–35)
- Sub-district 3 Chelsea North East (RG9 36–39).

Of all the registration districts across London, Hampstead is the most complete with a 98.5 per cent survival.

Ancestry lists missing section numbers on its website. Searching on the Discovery catalogue, using the keywords 'missing' or 'wanting' and restricting the search to the RG 9 code will identify the missing pieces with the names of the parishes affected.

This was the first census administered separately in Scotland. The new Registrar General had no experience of census administration and several householders experienced problems reading the schedules as they were either illiterate or Scots Gaelic speakers. Most people in the Highlands and Islands only spoke Gaelic. There was also some confusion among the registrars and the enumerators as to which columns should be completed. Thus not all schedules were properly filled in.[5]

1861 Census – Liverpool (Ref. RG9/2653/46 p.6). (© Crown Copyright Images reproduced by courtesy of The National Archives, London, England. www.NationalArchives.gov.uk & www.TheGenealogist.co.uk)

How to Use the Census Effectively

Sadly for George Graham, family historians and others have disproved his assurances in 1861 that the census would not be used 'for the gratification of curiosity'.

Enumerators often gave more information than was required in the CEBs. It is always worth paying close attention to the writing in all columns on the original image, rather than relying on a transcription. This example, from 211 Scotland Road, Liverpool (ref. RG9/2653/46, p.6) shows a John Bestwick, in whose birthplace column was written: 'Dead when Enumeration taken'. Other interesting remarks found in the online census entries can often be found in the occupation column.

There are separate crew lists for the Scottish and English/Welsh censuses. Where ancestors are not found on one, they may be on the other.

The use of the word 'gentleman' in censuses can be unclear. On Tuesday, 2 April, the *Bury and Norwich Post, and Suffolk Herald* wrote:

> We have seen one objection made to the particulars specified – namely, the suggestion that persons who have retired from business 'may be entered' as 'retired farmer', 'retired grocer', &c.: but if there be any parties who are not desirous of stating their former vocation it is open to them to describe themselves according to the sources from which their incomes are derived, or, we apprehend, as 'gentlemen'.[6]

This definition of 'gentleman' as a retired person adds to the description of a member of the upper middle classes, and someone who was not in work.

Taking it Further

The disability column was of great significance to the administrators, not least the great medical statistician William Farr. This census entry for the House of Industry for the Relief of the Poor of Douglas on the Isle of Man (ref. RG9/4419 f. 72) shows full use of the disability column, even though only 'blind' and 'deaf and dumb' inhabitants were to be recorded in this year. There is Jane Hampton, for example, a 39-year-old unmarried servant who was described as an 'Imbecile'. Annie Briggs, a 46-year-old unmarried cook, had been deaf and dumb from birth. In the case of Elizabeth Gorry, the schedule was incorrectly completed with her disability, 'Blind and imbecile' being written into the Occupation column. The disability column gives further details, informing that Gorry had experienced her disabilities 'from her Birth'.

This example, which is an institution schedule, highlights the changes in society since the introduction of workhouses and other houses of industry, particularly from the reforms of the Poor Law in 1834. No longer were the majority of those with disabilities cared for at home. More details can be found on the inhabitants of workhouses and asylums through admission and discharge registers, creed books, and collections of case notes or medical data. These are usually held at local record offices, but some for London have been uploaded to the Ancestry website.

The crew lists on this census can help to identify merchant seamen and Royal Navy ancestors. Service records for the Royal Navy are held at TNA. The continuous service engagement books from 1853 to 1872 can be found in reference ADM 139 at TNA or searched online via the Discovery search engine. Service records of RN officers and Royal Marines can also be searched online.

Merchant seamen records are held at The National Archives, although Lloyd's captains' registers are at the Guildhall Library. The National Archives' records of merchant navy seamen, which the central government created to monitor a potential reserve of sailors for the

1861 Census District House of Industry for the Relief of the Poor, Douglas (Ref. RG 9/4419/72 p.1). (© Crown Copyright Images reproduced by courtesy of The National Archives, London, England. www.NationalArchives.gov.uk & www.TheGenealogist. co.uk)

Royal Navy (1835–57) have been digitized at Findmypast. Details on the masters of ships may be found in the Lloyd's captains' registers (1851–1947), which are held at the London Metropolitan Archives. Certificate applications (1850–1927) by masters, mates, engineers and fishing officers are held at the National Maritime Museum, but have been digitized on Ancestry. Further sources relating to ships' crews can be found at the crew list website **www.crewlist.org.uk**, and for Welsh seamen at **www.welshmariners.org.uk**.

For seamen who were also serving before 1854, there is useful genealogical information in the Trinity House papers (1787–1854), which are held at the Society of Genealogists. Ancestors' names can be found in these via the calendars that have been digitized on Findmypast. These calendars are arranged alphabetically, but they cannot be searched by individuals. Searches can be made of a relevant digitized page in order to find a possible entry of an ancestor. The original papers comprise petitions submitted by the seaman or his widow and include details of apprenticeship, as well as baptism and marriage certificates.

Details of ships can be found at records held at TNA (such as ledgers, medical books and passenger lists), via newspaper reports, or at TheShipsList website, **www.theshipslist.com**. Records of ships of the Indian navy are held in the India Office records at the British Library.

Unique Features of the Non-English Censuses

In Scotland, the enumeration districts were based loosely on parishes. The returns are arranged by parish (each with its own parish number) and enumeration district. These parish numbers had been assigned in 1855, with the introduction of civil registration. The census report revealed that the population of Scotland, including the army, navy and merchant shipping in 1861, was 3,062,204. The total number of rooms with windows in Scotland was 1,708,405.

Once again, a separate Welsh-language schedule was available for households in Wales.

For Ireland, the following transcriptions of census records survive for 1861:

- Loughinisland, County Down (names all Presbyterians; in *Family Links* journal, 1 (6), September 1982, pp.5–11; 1 (7), January 1983, pp.9–14)
- Enniscorthy, County Wexford (names all Roman Catholics, NLI ref. P4250 N1391).

The household schedules for the 1861 Irish census were destroyed before 1922 by order of the government. Full census reports for Irish counties can be read at HISTPOP. The total population of Ireland on 8 April 1861 was 5,764,543; a decrease of 787,842 from the 1851 census, largely the result of mass emigration following the Great Famine.

Summary

Graham and Farr continued to maintain firm control over the census process. Medical statistics were as important to Farr as to earlier census administrators, and good progress was made in using them for the benefit of public health. Sadly, large numbers of deaths from infectious disease continued. Despite calls for a second religious census, only Ireland took a count of religious belief and attendance in 1861. Nonconformists were bolstered in the knowledge from 1851 that dissension was strong across England and, notably, Wales. Nonconformism continued to grow.

Scotland's first census after its introduction of civil registration is significant for family historians, as is the introduction of its own census administration. The Scottish census of this year is not as accurate as those of England and Wales, but it set a new precedent for Scottish administration. Separate crew lists and an army list compiled from non-census records are other useful features of 1861 records for family historians. The 1871 census would build upon this progress, and few changes would be introduced.

Chapter 6

1871: THE LAST CENSUS OVERSEEN BY GRAHAM AND FARR

Historical Context

KEY EVENTS OF 1861–1871
- 1861: Death of Prince Albert
- 1866: Liberal Party tries unsuccessfully to push through a parliamentary reform bill
- 1866: Cholera epidemic
- 1867: Disraeli's (Conservative) Reform Act extends the vote to more than 1.5 million men and includes every male adult householder and every male lodger who paid £10 per year for furnished rooms
- 1868–74: William Ewart Gladstone (1809–98) serves as Liberal prime minister
- 1869: Irish Land Act
- 1869: Irish Church Act: disestablishes the Irish Protestant Church
- 1870: Education Act creates school boards, leading to the building of board schools in areas of poor educational provision for the working classes and increases the provision of elementary education for all
- 1871: Trade Union Act: recognizes trade unions as legal entities, with protection for their funds
- 1871: Criminal Law Amendment Act makes picketing (by trade unions) illegal.

By the time of the 1871 census, the Liberal Party had been in power for more than two years. Infectious disease remained a problem for people across all social classes. The year leading up to the census of

1871 saw an epidemic of scarlet fever, and William Farr was, as always, keen to assess the health of the nation through the statistics revealed by the census. He had finally conceded defeat regarding his views on miasma theory after John Snow's report on the London cholera epidemic proved the link between the victims and infected water as opposed to air. However, the census statistics he shared with John Snow had helped in the latter's work on the epidemiology of cholera.

There was more to discover and prove through Farr's innovative use of statistics, a view shared by many of his contemporaries in 1871. The Liverpool Health Committee, for example, 'determined to make the most strenuous efforts to take the census accurately, so a hope was expressed that by establishing the soundness of the basis upon which the mortality figures were founded, public attention might give rise to a remedy for the extreme unhealthiness of the town'.[1] Increasingly, since the nervousness shown by some towards the census of 1841, newspapers and local authorities had shown strong support for census-taking. The benefits that the statistics might bring to specific parts of the nation were becoming clearer.

In 1870, the GRO approached the Local Government Board to pass the required Census Act. The Act, 33 & 34 Vict., c. 107, was passed on 10 August 1870. On the Channel Islands and the Isle of Man, the census was supervised by the respective lieutenant governors. The census of England and Wales was again overseen by a team in the census office at Craig's Court. Major George Graham, the Registrar General, and Dr William Farr, the Superintendent of Statistics, remained in charge of the process. Their long service to censuses brought a continuity, which was reflected in the similarity of this census to that of 1861. Graham and Farr were assisted in this year by James Thomas Hammick, a barrister, William Clode, secretary, Thomas Oakes, accountant, and Francis James Williams, chief clerk. The 625 superintendent registrars and 2,197 registrars worked to divide England and Wales into 33,000 enumeration districts. By now, payments to enumerators were well organized. They received a fixed sum of one guinea, plus two shillings and sixpence for every 100 persons in their district above the first 400 persons, sixpence for every mile they walked while delivering schedules beyond the first five, and a further sixpence per mile beyond the first five when collecting.[2]

The 1871 census took place on Sunday, 2 April. As usual, the enumerators delivered the household schedules in the week before census night and collected them on the Monday (3 April). Following this, the enumerators copied the details into the CEBs and sent them on to the census office. As for previous censuses, the household schedules for England, Wales and the islands have been destroyed, but the CEBs are held at The National Archives. These have been digitized by a number of website providers. The schedules and census reports reveal the population of 1871 to be 26,072,036, an increase of almost 6 million people from a decade earlier.

Despite the apparent efficiency of the census process, the GRO officers were not entirely happy with the quality of enumerators. A Treasury Committee to inquire into questions connected with the taking of the census was set up. Minutes of evidence, Appendices page ix, states:

> The evidence we have received as to the manner in which enumerators are selected and their work is performed, at any rate in England, has led us to wish it were possible to secure a better set of men than have hitherto been obtained. The selection now rests virtually with the registrars, and there is evidence that their choice is not always determined solely by reference to actual qualification to work… 'one unfortunate selection' was made in which a registrar appointed a newspaper seller who used to sell newspapers at the starting point of the South Hackney omnibuses, and who lost 'a number of his schedules on the day of the census…'

They had been keen to employ men who applied out of a sense of civic duty. Instead, the enumerators of 1871 came from a variety of backgrounds and some may have been motivated solely by money. It is possible that older men would employ an assistant to help deliver the schedules; they would pay for this themselves.

The fee had been increased after complaints from enumerators at a flat fee that took no account of the differences between districts. The fee per miles was only likely to be attractive to rural enumerators, but those in heavily populated urban areas could quickly earn extra payment for counting more than 400 people. Many enumerators were schoolmasters, such as William Edward Burcham, a 42-year-old government-certificated schoolmaster in the village of Galgate, Lancashire. In Compton Valence, Dorset, the enumerator was a 56-year-old organist and organ-builder named Joseph Baker Woodford, while district 15 of the industrial area of Sedgley, Staffordshire was enumerated by Thomas Turley, a 62-year-old iron master. The name of the enumerator of each district is found on the front page of the CEB, along with the description of the district. These pages have been digitized on Ancestry and can be found by clicking on 'Image 1' of each district.

What Details are Included?

For the most part, the questions asked in the 1871 census were the same as those for 1861. The options in the disability question were extended to include imbeciles, idiots and lunatics, as well as those who were deaf and dumb, and blind. Full descriptions outlining the definitions of these disabilities are found in the census report. For ships, the census covered British and, notably, foreign vessels. Those enumerated were those that had arrived in British ports between 25 March and 2 April. Other forms were given to ships arriving up to 2 May.

The enumerators' books asked for the civil parish, city or municipal borough, municipal ward, parliamentary borough, town, village or hamlet, local board and ecclesiastical district:

- ROAD, STREET, etc. and No. or NAME of HOUSE
- HOUSES Inhabited
  Uninhabited (U) or Building (B)
- NAME and Surname of each Person
- RELATION to Head of Family
- Condition
- AGE of Males
  Females
- Rank, profession or OCCUPATION
- WHERE BORN
- Whether
  (1) Deaf & Dumb
  (2) Blind
  (3) Imbecile or Idiot
  (4) Lunatic.

The summary tables in the enumerators' books included the following:

- Number of males and females temporarily absent, and the reasons for their absence
- Number of males and females temporarily present, and the reasons for their presence
- Number of schedules, houses (inhabited, uninhabited, being built), males and females in each named civil parish or township, or parts thereof
- Number of the household schedules filled in by the enumerator
- Number of elements in (3) on each page of the nominal returns.

Special returns existed for:

- Of the army, from his Royal Highness the Field-Marshal Commanding-in-Chief
- Of the navy, from the Lords Commissioners of the Admiralty
- Of merchant seamen on vessels in home ports, from the Honourable Board of Customs
- Of merchant seamen abroad, from the Registrar General of merchant seamen
- Of British subjects in foreign states, from the Secretary of State for Foreign Affairs
- Of British population in India, from the Secretary of State for India in Council
- Of population of British colonies, from the Secretary of State for the Colonies.

Although few changes were made to the main English and Welsh census schedule, a new approach was made to counting the population of the colonies and dependencies of the British Empire. In 1861, the statistics were drawn from a number of separate colonial censuses, which were taken on different dates. In 1871, a specific colonial census would be taken. Population figures for India, for example, were drawn from the quinquennial census of 1866–67. However, this count did not cover all parts of the country and did not include names or other details that would be of obvious use to family historians. The result of the overall count of the empire was 234,762,593 but it is unlikely that the full extent of imperial subjects was recorded.[3]

A further census was taken in India in 1872. The report, written by Henry Waterfield, *Memorandum on the Census of British India 1871–72* (Eyre and Spottiswoode, 1875) is available to read online at La Trobe University's website: **https://arrow.latrobe.edu.austore/3/4/5/5/2/public/pagec981.html**

The Scottish census requested the following:

THE UNDERMENTIONED HOUSES ARE SITUATE WITHIN THE BOUNDARIES OF THE PARISH OF / QUOAD SACRA PARISH OF / PARLIAMENTARY BURGH OF / ROYAL BURGH OF / TOWN OF / VILLAGE OF

- No. of Schedule
- ROAD, STREET, &c., and No. or NAME of HOUSE

- HOUSES Inhabited
  Uninhabited (U) or Building (B)
- NAME and Surname of each Person
- RELATION to Head of Family
- CONDITION
- ROYAL BURGH OF
- AGE of
  Males
  Females
- Rank, Profession, or OCCUPATION
- WHERE BORN
- Number of Children from 5 to 13 attending School or being educated at Home
- Rooms with One or more Windows
- Whether 1. Deaf and Dumb. 2. Blind. 3. Imbecile or Idiot. 4. Lunatic.

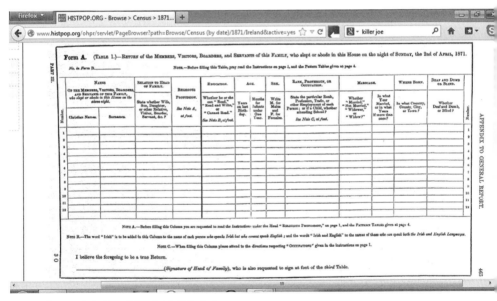

Screenshot of the 1871 Irish Schedule.

Form A of the Irish census was the return of the members, visitors, boarders and servants of this family, who slept or abode in the house on the night of Sunday, 2 April 1871:

- NAMES OF THE MEMBERS, VISITORS, BOARDERS, AND SERVANTS OF THIS FAMILY, who slept or abode in this house on the above night
  Christian Names
  Surnames
- RELATION TO HEAD OF FAMILY
  State whether Wife, Son, Daughter, or other Relative, Visitor, Boarder, Servant, &c.
- RELIGIOUS PROFESSION
- EDUCATION
  Whether he or she can 'Read', 'Read and Write,' or 'Cannot Read'
- AGE
  Years on last Birthday
  Months for Infants under One Year
- SEX
  Write M. for Males and F. for Females
- RANK, PROFESSION, OR OCCUPATION
  State the particular Rank, Profession, Trade, or other Employment of each Person; or if a Child, whether attending School?
- MARRIAGE
  Whether 'Married,' 'Not Married,' 'Widower,' or 'Widow'
  In what Year Married or in what Years if more than once?
- WHERE BORN
  In what Country, County, City, or Town?
- DEAF AND DUMB OR BLIND
  Whether Deaf and Dumb, or Blind?

Finding Aids[4]

Street and surname indexes are available at The National Archives and relevant local record offices.

Published indexes include those for Bethnal Green, Hackney, Mile End Old Town, Poplar, Shoreditch, St George in the East, Stepney and Whitechapel, produced by the East of London Family History Society.

Thirty-five Scottish street indexes can be searched at the NRS site: **https://www.nrscotland.gov.uk/research/guides/census-records/1871-census**

A census index for the 1871 census of Matlock with Matlock Bath, registration district of Bakewell, can be searched at **https://www.andrewsgen.com/matlock/c1871/index.htm**

Surname indexes for parishes in the area of Ingleborough, Yorkshire can be searched under census/registers at at **http://www.ingleborougharchaeology.org.uk/**

Surname indexes for Veryan in Cornwall are online at **http://freepages. rootsweb.com/~dtrounce/genealogy/veryanlists4.html**

The National Archives' code for this census is RG 10.

Online Resources

TheGenealogist offers a separate crew list search. The advanced options allow a search of forename, surname, age (+/- 5 years), vessel name, rank or occupation, and birth county.

Other census searches on TheGenealogist include the master search and the county search. The advanced search options for the county include forename, surname, age, district, relationship to head of household, birthplace/county, occupation and street address.

Findmypast allows a search by person or by address. The person search (advanced) includes the options of first name(s), last name, sex, birth place, birth year, country, county, marriage condition, registration district, civil parish, municipal borough, ward, parliamentary borough, town or village, ecclesiastical parish, relationship to head of household, and other persons in same household. A search by the census reference is also available.

Ancestry has a general search which covers most of its databases. The 1871 census can be searched via a dedicated webpage. The search can be narrowed to Channel Islands, England, Isle of Man, Scotland and Wales. The advanced search includes first and middle name(s), last name, birth year and location, lived in, any event year, family member and gender. It also has a 'more' option for searching with a keyword such as an occupation or, for example, 'inmate' for a resident of an institution.

MyHeritage offers a search by name, birth year and place, residence and keyword. Advanced search options include birth date, names of relatives, and image reference.

Free Resources

The indexes on Ancestry and Findmypast are free.

The FreeCen website provides links to transcriptions of census data for some parishes in the following counties:

Aberdeenshire	Caernarvonshire	County Durham
Anglesey	Caithness	East Riding of Yorkshire
Argyllshire	Carmarthenshire	Essex
Berkshire	Cornwall	Flintshire
Buckinghamshire	Denbighshire	Glamorgan
Bute	Dorset	Herefordshire

Hertfordshire	Norfolk	Suffolk
Huntingdonshire	North Riding of	Somerset
Kent	Yorkshire	Surrey
Kinross-shire	Nottinghamshire	Sussex
Leicestershire	Oxfordshire	Warwickshire
Lincolnshire	Peeblesshire	Westmoreland
London	Renfrewshire	Wigtownshire
Merionethshire	Rutland	Wiltshire
Monmouthshire	Scottish shipping	West Riding of
Morayshire	Selkirkshire	Yorkshire
Nairnshire	Shropshire	

FamilySearch offers a free image browse of this census.

Problems
Known missing parts of the 1871 census include the following:

- Piece 3278: St Margaret, Leicester
- Piece 4213: Preston
- Piece 4729: Eastoft and Haldenby
- Piece 5444: Llangyfelach, Penderry and Llandilotalybont, Glamorganshire
- Piece 5463: Porteynon, Penrice, Oxwich, Nicholaston, Penmaen, Reynoldston, Llandewy and Knelston in Glamorganshire (registration sub-district 2B, Gower Western)
- Piece 5590: Talgarth, Gryne-fawr and Grwyne-fechan, Breconshire.

To find the missing parts listed on The National Archives website, search the Discovery catalogue with the keywords 'missing' or 'wanting', with the census reference RG 10.

How to Use the Census Effectively
This page from a CEB for Spring Bank in the municipal ward of North Myton in Hull gives an indication of what can be found in this census.

The first entries on this page are for the del Banco family. Hull was a thriving port in 1871 and had a high level of immigration, particularly from Eastern Europe. Despite his Italian-sounding name, the head of the household Cesar del Banco was from Hamburg in the recently unified Germany. His wife Clare was a local woman from nearby Goole. Cesar worked as a fruit merchant and was prosperous enough to employ a domestic servant, 15-year-old Fanny Oliver. Fanny had perhaps been

1871 Census entry for Kingston upon Hull, Yorkshire, District 22 (Ref. RG10/4791/81 p. 1). (© Crown Copyright Images reproduced by courtesy of The National Archives, London, England. www.NationalArchives.gov.uk & www.TheGenealogist.co.uk)

employed because there was a new baby in the house, recorded as 'under 2 Months'.

Their neighbours in Zoological Terrace, Spring Bank include a 42-year-old merchant and commission agent from Hull, a 42-year-old furniture broker, also from Hull and the Norfolk-born publican of Spring Bank's public house, the 'Polar Bear'. Interestingly, the publican was a married woman, Jane Story.

Her husband Charles, who was twelve years younger, appeared to work outside of the pub as a plumber and gas-fitter.

The last entry on the page is for the inhabitants of the Hull Seaman's General Orphan Asylum. The first entries include the certificated teacher from Liverpool, his wife, the asylum's matron, along with a schoolmistress, cook and laundress. The first child to be named was William N. Carlile, age 13, who had been born in Hull and is described as 'Seaman's Son'.

The inclusion of the asylum shows how institutions were enumerated alongside domestic properties in this census.

Examining the neighbouring properties and households in the area where an ancestor lived can provide useful social detail. The social class of others in the area can provide insight into possible clientele where your ancestor ran a business. The close presence of pubs, shops, theatres or coffee houses may suggest establishments frequented by your ancestors. To be clear as to how close the respective residences were to each other, local maps should be consulted. Further details may also be found in rate books. Surviving volumes are held at local record offices, often on microfilm.

The National Archives' registration district historical maps can be seen online at **www.cassinimaps.co.uk/shop/tna1.asp?id=166&page=ce**.

Interesting regional aspects of the census can be found in contemporary local newspapers. The *Hampshire Advertiser*[5] contains a report from Yarmouth on the Isle of Wight, in which

> We are informed by Mr. Salter, the census enumerator, that in the population of 810 there are no less than 182 children who go to school, besides which 12 are educated at home. There are 4 males above the age of 80, their united ages being 337. The oldest man is 87, and the oldest woman 88. There are 5 men and women between the ages of 70 and 80, the united ages of the former being 369 and the latter 663. One facetious tradesman returned the occupation of his son (3 years old) as 'all kinds of mischief,' and in another house the inmates entered on the census paper the name of a person then lying dead at the time in the house.

Frederick Salter wrote the description of the enumeration district from the copy supplied by the registrar. The first column reads:

> Yarmouth Parish
> The whole of the Parish of Yarmouth
> Comprising the Whole of the Town of Yarmouth within the Boundaries of the Ancient Borough and Corporation including the Highway, Toll House and the YarBridge, Toll House, the Castle Gas Works and all houses in the Parish and District.

A similar assessment of other enumeration districts can be made by close inspection of the census returns on the online databases.

Taking it Further

Besides exploring the neighbours and local leisure sites in ancestors' localities, further investigation can be made into the history of the region using local history books and resources.

One useful website for this is British History Online at **www.british-history.ac.uk**, which provides access to hundreds of primary and secondary records. These include the *The Victoria History of the Counties of England*, English Heritage's *Survey of London*, Blomefield's *History of Norfolk*, Mackenzie's *Newcastle-upon-Tyne* and Ordnance Survey maps.

Follow up on Welsh ancestors by searching Welsh Newspapers Online at **https://newspapers.library.wales**

Unique Features of the Non-English Censuses

For Wales, the CEBs were completed in English even where Welsh-language household schedules had been used. From 1871, the enumerators were required to write a 'W' in the first column of the CEB to indicate where a Welsh schedule had been used. Family historians can use these 'W's to identify whether their ancestors in Wales spoke Welsh.

Although destruction of official copies of the 1871 Irish census was authorized by the government before 1911, a few locally retained unofficial transcripts remain.

Transcripts of the Drumcondra and Loughbracken, County Meath census for 1871 were retained in the Catholic parish registers. This can be seen on microfilm, reference P4184 and N1325, at the NLI. Details of the census are online at the Irish Ancestors website **https://www.irishancestors.ie/resources/unique-resources/drumcondra-loughbrackan-1871-census-fragment/**

In Scotland for this census, ancient county names were used by some enumerators. The affected counties, with modern equivalents, are as follows:[6]

Ancient County	Modern Name
Kincardineshire	Edinburghshire
	Midlothian
	Haddingtonshire
	East Lothian
	Linlithgowshire
	West Lothian
	Forfarshire
	Angus
Elginshire	Morayshire
	Tweeddale
	Peeblesshire
	Liddesdale
	Roxburghshire
Gallowayshire	Western District – Wigtownshire
	Eastern District – Kirkcudbright

Summary

The 1871 census took place against a background of a Liberal government and major social reforms. The empire was firmly established in India, the West Indies and Australasia, and the government used the statistics of population counting to affirm Britain's increasingly confident position on the world stage. Epidemics continued, although reduced, particularly in the case of cholera, as a result of John Snow's work. Dr William Farr had to concede that his theory of illness caused by miasma was wrong, again proved by Snow's work with cholera. Farr had made a major contribution to the census over his decades as commissioner. Thanks both to him and Major Graham the census now ran smoothly, the public on the whole co-operated with their enumerators, and it was popular with the press and regional officials. For these reasons, the census had become a reliable tool for social, family and local history.

By 1881, a new team would be running the census, with change the inevitable result. In the present day, the 1881 census is of central importance to family historians and is one of the best-indexed and most-researched censuses produced in the United Kingdom.

Chapter 7

1881: THE FIRST CENSUS TO BE USED BY FAMILY HISTORIANS

Historical Context

KEY EVENTS OF 1871–1881
- 1875: Charles Stewart Parnell (1846–91) becomes leader of the Irish Parliamentary Party
- 1876–9: William Malachi Burke (1819–79) serves as Registrar General for Ireland
- 1879: Thomas Wrigley Grimshaw (1839–1900) succeeds Dr William Malachi Burke as Registrar General of Ireland
- 1880: Brydges Henniker (1835–1906) is appointed Registrar General
- 1880–05: William Gladstone serves as prime minister (the second of his four terms of office)
- 1880: Parnell becomes MP for the city of Cork
- 1881: Stair Agnew (1831–1916) is appointed Registrar General of Scotland
- 1881: Irish Coercion Bills enact the temporary suspension of *habeas corpus*
- 1881: War with Boers (First Boer War) ends in South Africa
- 1881: death of the former prime minister, Benjamin Disraeli, Earl of Beaconsfield, Conservative leader
- 1881: Robert Cecil, the Marquess of Salisbury, succeeds Disraeli as leader of the Conservative Party in the House of Lords
- 1881: Sir Stafford Northcote succeeds as leader of the Conservative Party in the House of Commons.

In Ireland, the political situation had intensified since January, with the enactment of the all-too-frequent Irish Coercion Bills. Gladstone was desperate to create peace, but landlords were evicting tenant farmers in their thousands. After Charles Parnell led tenants to rise up against their landlords, the agitation resulted in widespread violence. Despite this, census-collecting took place in Ireland much as it had in previous decades. Ireland's Registrar General was now based at Charlemont House in Rutland (later Parnell) Square, Dublin. Today this is the home of Dublin City Gallery.

Across the Irish Sea, Stair Agnew (1831–1916) was appointed Registrar General of Scotland on 13 January, replacing William Pitt Dundas. For the 1881 census, Agnew was assisted by Dr William Robertson and Dr R.J. Blair Cunynghame.

Developments had taken place in education: with the passing of Sandon's 1876 Elementary Education Act, school attendance committees had been set up. Despite this, as responsibility for ensuring attendance had been given to parents, examples of child labour remained. Parents, wary of revealing their child's work activities, may have described them on the census as 'scholar'. Family historians should therefore check for evidence of school attendance in the admission, discharge and creed registers that exist at the relevant local record office.

Nonconformism continued to be popular. Teetotalism, or temperance, a movement closely associated with Nonconformists, was also growing. On 27 March 1881, only a few days before the census took place, the Riot Act was read in Basingstoke, where troops were called to calm a confrontation between the Salvation Army and more than 2,000 supporters of the alcohol trade, who were armed with sticks and other weapons. The Salvation Army had arrived in Basingstoke with demands of 'Ban all drink!' This was met with angry responses from the regulars of the town's inns and hostelries, who took part in a series of attacks on the Salvationists that culminated in the riot of the 27th. The leaders of the riots were later imprisoned. Both the Salvation Army and alcohol remained in Basingstoke.

Perhaps the two best-known teetotallers in Britain in 1881 were William (1829–1912) and Catherine Booth (1829–90), who had founded the Salvation Army three years earlier in 1878. In 1879, the first Habitual Drunkards Act was passed. Teetotallers and Nonconformists would be celebrating later that year in August when the Sunday Closing (Wales) Act passed, leading to the prohibition of the sale of alcohol in Wales on Sundays. The Act was repealed in 1961, although some counties remained 'dry' until as recently as 1996. One of the largest set of temperance records in the UK, the Livesey Collection, is held at the University of Central Lancashire in Preston. Further details can be found at **www.uclan.ac.uk/ students/library/livesey_collection.php**.

The Census Act (43 & 44 Vict., c. 37) was passed on 7 September 1880. A new Registrar General, Sir Brydges Powell Henniker (1835–1906), Baronet, would be overseeing the 1881 census following the resignation of Major George Graham in 1879. Dr William Farr had also resigned in 1879. His position of Superintendent of Statistics was taken in 1880 by Dr William Ogle (1827–1912). In the same year, Ogle published the *Annual Report of the Registrar General*, which included work on smallpox and vaccination as well as suicides. The following year he reported on inadequate certification of the causes of death, something with which many family historians are familiar. As Ogle was cautious about extending the census questions, the new census included few changes.

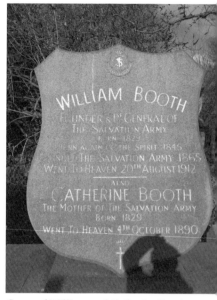

Grave of William and Catherine Booth.

Higgs has noted the reduced size of the reports under Henniker and Ogle (published 1881 and 1883), in comparison with those of Graham and Farr. Nevertheless, some additions were made. The census reports for this year were the first to make use of the sanitary districts, which had been created by the Public Health Acts of 1874 and 1875. These were divided into urban sanitary districts and rural sanitary districts and are often abbreviated on birth, marriage and death certificates to USD and RSD. The districts were controlled by sanitary authorities, who oversaw sewers, drinking water, slums and street-cleaning. In Ireland, sanitary districts were set up in 1878 following the Public Health (Ireland) Act. No sanitary districts were established in Scotland.

Despite Farr's celebrated work on the census and his endeavours as a medical statistician and epidemiologist, outbreaks of infectious disease continued to occur. On census night, a smallpox epidemic was raging among London's poor:

At Homerton 70 patients had been admitted in the fortnight; seven had died, 64 had been discharged, 111 were still under treatment, and nine beds were available. At Fulham 99 had been admitted, 11 had died, 63 had been discharged, 245 were still under treatment, and 27 beds were available. At Deptford 190 had been admitted, 33 had died, 155 had been discharged, 388 were under treatment, and 12 beds were available. The totals were 378 admitted in the fortnight, 61 deaths, 319 discharged, 881 under treatment (an increase of 19 on the previous return), and 49 beds available as against 68 a fortnight ago. The totals of the fever return showed a decline of 52 cases in the metropolis from the numbers a fortnight ago.[1]

Once again enumerators delivered the schedules in the week leading up to census night, collecting them the next day, when they were sent on to Somerset House. The efficiency of census-taking was by now so well established that *The Times* remarked, 'The celerity and smoothness of the enumeration mark the perfection of modern administrative machinery.'[2] The census, it argued, was a true symbol of Victorian efficiency.

The Times went on to sum up the continued purpose of the census:

> The REGISTRAR-GENERAL will in a few hours have the means of discovering how industry has faded away from one division of the land, how it has thriven or revived in another. He will be able to ascertain to what extent its confluence in this district has compensated for its subsidence in that. The ebb and flow of favour in the direction of different callings will read important lessons. The aggregate of human beings at the several periods of existence will show how disease and poverty had their will in one season, how health and trade supplied the gaps in those which succeeded.

What Details are Included?

The census of 1881 was taken on Sunday, 3 April and would reveal another increase in the British population. The total now stood at 29,707,207, with an English and Welsh population of 25,974,000.

This census continued to use the same columns as in 1871. In the enumerators' books, the units were divided into civil parish (or township), city or municipal borough, municipal ward, parliamentary borough, town or village or hamlet, urban sanitary district, rural sanitary district and ecclesiastical parish or district:

- ROAD, STREET, &c. and No. or NAME of HOUSE
- HOUSES Inhabited
  Uninhabited (U), or Building (B)
- NAME and Surname of each Person
- RELATION to Head of Family
- CONDITION as to Marriage

- AGE last Birthday of
  Males
  Females
- Rank, Profession, or OCCUPATION
- WHERE BORN
- Whether (1) Deaf & Dumb, (2) Blind, (3) Imbecile or Idiot, (4) Lunatic.

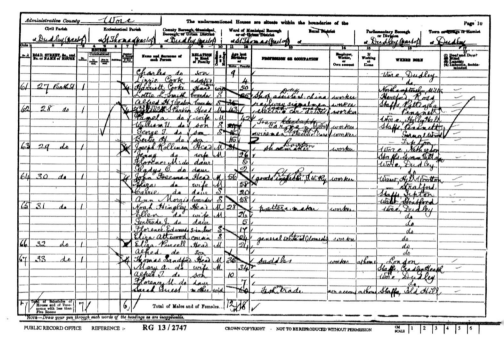

1901 Census showing the Hingley Family (Ref. RG13/ 2747/9 p. 10). (© Crown Copyright Images reproduced by courtesy of The National Archives, London, England. www.NationalArchives.gov.uk & www.TheGenealogist.co.uk)

The institution and merchant vessels were identified in the census reports as follows:

- Barracks and military quarters
- HM ships at home
- Workhouses (including pauper schools)
- Hospitals (sick, convalescent, incurable)
- Lunatic asylums (public and private)
- Prisons
- Certified reformatories and industrial schools
- Merchant vessels
- Schools.

The summary tables in the enumerators' books included the following:

- Number of males and females temporarily absent, and the reasons for their absence
- Number of males and females temporarily present, and the reasons for their presence
- Number of schedules, houses (inhabited, uninhabited, being built), males and females in each named civil parish or township, or parts thereof
- As above for other administrative areas
- Number of elements in (3) on each page of the nominal returns.

The Scottish census requested the following:

The undermentioned Houses are situate within the Boundaries of the Civil Parish of/Quoad Sacra Parish of/School Board District of/Parliamentary Burgh of/Royal Burgh of/Police Burgh of/Town of/Village or Hamlet of

- No. of Schedule
- ROAD, STREET, &c., and No. or NAME of HOUSE
- HOUSES Inhabited
  Uninhabited (U) or Building (B)
- NAME and Surname of each Person
- RELATION to Head of Family
- CONDITION
- AGE of
- Rank, Profession, or OCCUPATION
- WHERE BORN
- Whether 1. Deaf and Dumb. 2. Blind. 3. Imbecile or Idiot. 4. Lunatic
- Rooms with One or more Windows.

Finding Aids

Street indexes are held at The National Archives for all metropolitan districts and districts with a population of more than 40,000. Local street indexes are available at relevant record offices and archives. The Society of Genealogists' library holds the *Census & Index for 1841–1901 Eydon, Northamptonshire*, a CD-ROM of the census for *Cheslyn Hay & Great Wyrley* in Staffordshire, the *Census for Shareshill, Hilton & Saredon 1841–1901* (also in Staffordshire), and the *Census Reports of Ireland, County Limerick*.

The British Library provides access to the census via Findmypast

The 1881 census tracts for the parish of Veryan in Cornwall are at **http://freepages.rootsweb.com/~dtrounce/genealogy/veryanlists5.html**.

A census database for the area around Metheringham, Lincolnshire can be searched at **www.macla.co.uk/census.htm**.

Online Resources

The first UK census index to appear online was that for 1881. The census had been indexed and transcribed by the Church of Jesus Christ of Latter-Day Saints for a CD-ROM that was published in 1999. The transcriptions were uploaded to the FamilySearch website in 2003 and can be searched free of charge. This original CD-ROM transcription continues to be regarded as the most accurate of the 1881 census and is used by other online providers, including Ancestry.

The National Archives digitized the census returns of 1881 and launched them online in 2004 in association with Ancestry. Ancestry allows transcriptions of the 1881 census only (England, Wales and Islands in the British Seas) to be searched for free. A search can be made through the general 'search all records' option. Otherwise, on the 1881 census page, advanced search options include first and middle name, last name, birth year and location, lived in, any event year and location, family member (choose from drop-down box), keyword and gender. The transcription gives details of name, age, relation to head of household, spouse's name, gender, where born, civil parish, county/island, country, sometimes street address, condition as to marriage, registration district, sub-registration district, EU/institution/vessel, piece, folio, page numbers and the names and ages of other household members. These can then be clicked on for further details.

TheGenealogist must be searched by surname, along with either a forename or an age. The 'master census transcript search' is available, or a search of the 1881 census can be made through the county option. Name variants include nicknames and phonetically matched surnames. Advanced search options include street address, occupation, birthplace/county, relation to head of the household, and district. The transcript includes the address and registration district, surname, forename, age, relation to head of the household, occupation, birthplace and image reference.

Findmypast also has a free transcript search of the 1881 England and Wales census, but there is a fee for the Scottish census. Images are unavailable for the Scottish census. The transcription includes details of first name, middle name, last name, sex, birthplace, age, place of residence, county and relationship to head of household. The person search includes first name, last name, birth year, occupation, birthplace, place of residence, country, county and the names of other people in the same household. An address search is available, using all or part of the street name. A separate search can be made using the full census reference, if known.

MyHeritage offers a basic search by name, birth year and place, residence and keyword. Its advanced search includes exact birth date, names of relatives, and image reference.

GenesReunited offers a search of this census by forename, surname, year of birth, place keywords and other forenames in the household. The transcribed details give further information, such as marital status, address and occupation. The original document can also be viewed.

RootsUK is provided by TheGenealogist and can be searched by forename and surname, although unregistered users can search on surname only.

The digitized images of the 1881 census for Scotland can be viewed only at the ScotlandsPeople website. The other census database providers offer transcriptions only. However, the LDS transcription is more detailed than that offered on the ScotlandsPeople site. For this reason, although the 1881 census search on ScotlandsPeople cannot be searched by address, the 1881 (LDS) census search on the same website can. Other search options include census place and birthplace. The search option is best done using street name or house name, leaving off street, road or lane if unsure.

Free Resources

The indexes on Ancestry and Findmypast are free. All available data on the FamilySearch website is free.

The FreeCen website provides links to transcriptions of census data for some parishes in the following counties:

- Caithness
- Cornwall.

Problems

Missing pieces for this census include the following:

- Piece 693: House numbers 17–22 Cunard Street, Camberwell, London
- Registration District 555: Returns for 36 persons on board 7 vessels at Gateshead

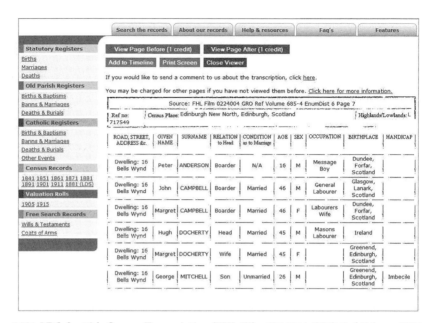

| | | Search the records | About our records | Help & resources | Faq's | Features |

Statutory Registers
Births
Marriages
Deaths
Old Parish Registers
Births & Baptisms
Banns & Marriages
Deaths & Burials
Catholic Registers
Births & Baptisms
Banns & Marriages
Deaths & Burials
Other Events
Census Records
1841 1851 1861 1871 1881
1891 1901 1911 1881 (LDS)
Valuation Rolls
1905 1915
Free Search Records
Wills & Testaments
Coats of Arms

View Page Before (1 credit)   View Page After (1 credit)
Add to Timeline   Print Screen   Close Viewer

If you would like to send a comment to us about the transcription, click here.

You may be charged for other pages if you have not viewed them before. Click here for more information.

Source: FHL Film 0224004 GRO Ref Volume 685-4 EnumDist 6 Page 7

Ref no: 717549   Census Place: Edinburgh New North, Edinburgh, Scotland   Highlands/Lowlands: L

ROAD, STREET, ADDRESS &c.	GIVEN NAME	SURNAME	RELATION to Head	CONDITION as to Marriage	AGE	SEX	OCCUPATION	BIRTHPLACE	HANDICAP
Dwelling: 16 Bells Wynd	Peter	ANDERSON	Boarder	N/A	16	M	Message Boy	Dundee, Forfar, Scotland	
Dwelling: 16 Bells Wynd	John	CAMPBELL	Boarder	Married	46	M	General Labourer	Glasgow, Lanark, Scotland	
Dwelling: 16 Bells Wynd	Margret	CAMPBELL	Boarder	Married	46	F	Labourers Wife	Dundee, Forfar, Scotland	
Dwelling: 16 Bells Wynd	Hugh	DOCHERTY	Head	Married	45	M	Masons Labourer	Ireland	
Dwelling: 16 Bells Wynd	Margret	DOCHERTY	Wife	Married	45	F		Greenend, Edinburgh, Scotland	
Dwelling: 16 Bells Wynd	George	MITCHELL	Son	Unmarried	26	M		Greenend, Edinburgh, Scotland	Imbecile

1881 LDS Scottish Census Transcription (FHL Film 0224004 GRO Ref Volume 6854 EnumDist 6 Page 7) for Marg[a]ret Campbell; Transcription on the ScotlandsPeople website. (Reproduced with the kind permission of the Registrar General for Scotland)

- Registration District 315: Returns for 10 persons on board 3 vessels at Banwell, Weston-super-Mare
- Registration District 496: Returns for 3 persons on board 2 vessels at Brighouse, Hipperholme with Brighouse
- Registration District 189: Returns for 7 persons on board 1 vessel at Rainham, Romford
- Registration District 629: Conway for 95 persons on board 13 vessels.

For a full list of parts missing from this census, search on TNA's Discovery catalogue, using the keywords 'missing' or 'wanting', using the census reference RG 11.

Accuracy had improved hugely since the census had begun, and even since names were introduced in the 1841 census. However, the statistics continued to highlight errors. Page 23 of the census report revealed that there were 61,064 more wives than there were husbands.[3]

How to Use the Census Effectively

Teetotal institutions, such as temperance halls, are recorded in this census and can be identified through keyword or sometimes address options via the online databases. Homes for 'inebriates', run by the Salvation Army and other groups, are also noted. The inebriated inmates were admitted when suffering addiction to alcohol, morphine or opium/laudanum. Records of drunkards convicted in London can be found on Findmypast, and from Birmingham on Ancestry.

It is important to be wary of details revealed in the census. Check for further records on the Hospital Records Database **www.nationalarchives. gov.uk/hospitalrecords**. Not all 'homes for inebriates' were genuine. In the ecclesiastical district of St Mary Newington, the enumerator visited the Ebenezer Terrace Home for Inebriate Women.[4] The census entry shows that the home was run by a 51-year-old master from Prussia, Charles Zierenberg and his wife, Wilhelmina, the 'Lady Superior'. They were assisted by a chaplain and a team of one matron and three under-matrons. The inmates included women as young as 14, like Louisa Lott from Old Ford, and 15, like Emily Kingston from Newington. Several, like Mary Clifford from Greenwich, were just 16. In 1893, the Zierenbergs launched a libel case against a journalist, Mr Labouchere, who claimed that the lady superior was taking destitute women, many not addicts, and forcing them to work for no pay in a laundry. The ensuing court case proved the Zierenbergs to be greedy fraudsters. The home was turned into a commercial laundry, which then provided many of the former inmates with paid work. The legal reports of the case can be read at The National Archives (ref. HO 45/9878/B15479).

Census returns for shipping in British waters recorded the names of all crew members, including Indian lascars and others born outside Britain. Passengers on some vessels are also included. Ships' schedules were handed out between 4 April and 3 May. Fishing vessels received their schedules up to 15 April.

Taking it Further

The 1881 census has been used by family historians, demographers and academics to map surnames.[5] These maps show statistics of surnames and geography. They have been used not only to mark the concentration of surnames by place for a given date but also to investigate the origins of names. The use of surname mapping was introduced by Kevin Schürer, the director of the UK data archive at the University of Essex. His work on the 1881 census revealed that 40 per cent of Britons shared 500 different surnames. At the other end of the scale, 10 per cent of the population shared 30,000 surnames.

The Ancestry database shows name distributions for different surnames. This offers a simple surname search of either the full or partial name, using a map of England and Wales based on the census of 1891, or of Scotland for the censuses of 1841–1901. The site provides maps showing the concentration of surnames. TheGenealogist provides surname concentration maps, created by a surname search, for the 1841–1901 censuses.

Offline, Stephen Archer's 'British 19th Century Surname Atlas' is software (available from **www.archersoftware.co.uk**) that generates a map, arranged by county or poor law unions, that shows the concentration of surnames. Ancestry's surname search includes a name-distribution feature, which maps surnames by county using data from the 1891 England and Wales, and Scotland censuses.

Unique Features of the Non-English Censuses

If you know where your Irish ancestors were living at the time of this census, it is worth reading through the relevant section of the census report. Although no parts of the census survive, the general report for Ireland 1881 gives detailed insight into the details returned. The last section includes maps and diagrams, which provide useful information on population, children in education, the classes of houses, literacy levels and agricultural factors. This is useful for researching the local and social history of the village or urban area of specific ancestors. Identifying tenant farmers or landlords from other sources and researching further with local newspapers and legal documents could help discover the role played by ancestors who lived in Ireland during the 1881 land disputes.

1881 Census entry showing Welsh Speakers. (© Crown Copyright Images reproduced by courtesy of The National Archives, London, England. www.NationalArchives.gov.uk & www.TheGenealogist.co.uk)

Unlike the English census, the Irish version asked occupants for their religious professions. This is broken down in the report by county and province. In Tipperary, for example, the population of 1881 comprised 94.2 per cent Roman Catholics, 5.1 per cent Protestant Episcopalians, 0.3 per cent Presbyterians, 0.3 per cent Methodists and 0.1 per cent 'all other denominations'. Besides the disabilities covered in England, the Irish census also asked for numbers of the sick in their own homes. The reports can be read in full at the HISTPOP website.

As with the 1871 census, in Wales the enumerators were required to write a 'W' in the first column of the CEB to indicate that a Welsh schedule had been used. In this example from School Street, Henllan, St Asaph, Denbighshire (ref. RG11/5532, p. 298), the first column includes two 'W's, indicating two Welsh-speaking households at numbers 59 (10 School Street) and 60 (14 School Street) on the schedule. The languages spoken can be confirmed if the householders are found on later censuses of Welsh speakers. Those using the Welsh schedules in this example are 57-year-old farm carter Evan Jones and his 22-year-old unemployed housemaid daughter, Anne Jones, and the family of Edward Evans, 56-year-old farm bailiff from Henllan. This includes his wife, Eunice Evans, a 50-year-old shopkeeper from Llannefydd in Denbighshire, his stepdaughter, Myfanwy Thomas, aged 19, and his daughter Margaret Ethel Evans, a 13-year-old scholar. Myfanwy worked with her mother in the shop and both girls were born in Henllan.

Others on the census of Wales who used Welsh as their first language may not have needed the separate schedule as they could read and write English as well. Ability to speak English and/or Welsh would be noted in future censuses.

On the Scottish census, an extra question was added in red after printing. In the 'where born' column, householders were to enter 'GAELIC' if they spoke the language 'habitually'.

Summary

The year 1881 was one of change, both within the census office and without. The great innovators and supporters of the Victorian census, Graham and Farr, had resigned, leaving less experienced men in charge. Nonconformity and teetotalism showed a marked increase in this year, not least as a result of the recent creation of the apparently fearless Salvation Army. Although census-taking appeared to run smoothly, inaccuracies and problems remained. However, for family historians, this census and its transcriptions remain one of the most accurate, and thus extremely useful for research.

Chapter 8

1891: THE INTRODUCTION OF ROOMS AND EMPLOYMENT STATUS TO THE CENSUS

Historical Context

KEY EVENTS OF 1881–1891
- 1881: Second Land Act (Gladstone's Act) passed: aimed to reduce Irish tenants' rents through the mediation of a land commission, and enabled some to buy their farms
- 1881: Charles Parnell is arrested for signing a 'no-rent manifesto' and encouraging tenant farmers across Ireland to strike
- 1885–86: Robert Cecil, 3rd Marquess of Salisbury, serves as prime minister
- 1885: Housing of the Working Classes Act, part of the Public Health Acts
- 1886: Protests at growing unemployment
- 1886–92: Lord Salisbury serves a second time as prime minister
- 1887: More violent protests over unemployment
- 1887: GRO survey
- 1888: Matchgirls' Strike: girls working for Bryant and May, the London-based makers of safety matches, mount a strike for improved work conditions
- 1889: London Dock Strike: dockworkers demand an increase in pay from 5d to 6d per hour, the 'docker's tanner'
- 1891: London–Paris telephone system, which operated via the first cross-Channel telephone cable, opened to the public
- 1891: Death of Charles Stewart Parnell.

The 1891 census was taken on Sunday, 5 April. Only a month earlier, Britain had been hit by the 'Great Blizzard'. Nottinghamshire experienced snowfall as early as Tuesday, 3 March, when for a short period from mid-morning, the area of Worksop and North Nottinghamshire 'was almost in total darkness'.[1]

By Monday the 9th, the storm had spread and ship passages were cancelled. A fisherman was drowned off Hastings, and Sussex in general was hit hard by the wind and snow: 'In the Beachy Head district the storm raged with great fury, the Channel being almost darkened by the falling snow during most of the afternoon.'[2]

A pensioner, James Bennett of Dowlais near Merthyr, died from exposure as he tried to walk home in the blizzard.[3] The storm particularly hit Wiltshire, South Wales, Somerset, Orkney and Newcastle, where work in the shipyards was suspended. The South and Wales were worst affected by the gales, but the snow caused problems nationwide. Railways and roads were blocked, and in London cabs were difficult to find (for those who could afford them). The *Daily News* reported, 'In London the thermometer did not exceed 39 deg. [4 degrees Celsius], and the weather was therefore about ten degrees colder than usual for the time of year.'[4]

On Saturday, 19 March 1887, the GRO had undertaken its own survey of the employment of around 30,000 working-class men in certain parts of London. These areas were St George in the East, parts of Battersea, Hackney and Deptford. Enumerators, under the employ of Sir Brydges Henniker, asked the manual labourers for their name, address, county of birth, marital condition, age, how long resident, if family resident, number of rooms occupied, weekly rent, if physically equal to ordinary labour, disabled, in or out of work, weekly wages, time since employment, cause of non-employment, means of subsistence when unemployed, length of time unemployed since 31 October, what members of family assist with income, the weekly amount of such subsistence and the name/relationship to the head of the household. The GRO obtained the results on behalf of the local government board. The results, recorded on more than 30,000 individual cards, were reported in *Conditions of the working classes. Tabulation of the statements made by men living in certain selected districts of London in March 1887* (BPP, 1887), LXXI.[5] One of the obvious flaws with this survey as a representation of working-class employment at this time is that it did not include women.

The results divided the male workers into the following thirty-five trade groups:

Clerks, travellers

Carmen, carters

Cabmen, etc.

Servants, etc.

Shopmen, etc.

Bakers

Butchers

Tailors

Bootmakers

Watchmakers, etc.

Machine-makers, etc.

Blacksmiths, etc.

Printers, etc.

Carpenters, etc.

Coopers

Shipwrights, etc.

Masons, bricklayers, etc.

Painters, plumbers, etc.

Wheelwrights, etc.

Cabinet-makers, etc.

Furriers, etc.

Sugar-bakers, refiners

Tobacco workers

Policemen

Seamen, etc.

Railwaymen except
   drivers, porters

Porters

Engine drivers

Unskilled labourers

Dockers

Hawkers,
   costermongers

Messengers,
   watchmen, etc.

Postmen, other
   government service

Artisans (undefined)

Nondescripts

Between 1881 and 1891, local boundaries were altered and new administrative counties were created by a series of Acts: the Local Government Act of 1888 and the Divided Parishes and Poor Law Amendment Act of 1882.[6] These created new counties for administrative purposes and divided some parishes. For the 631 registration districts of the 1891 census, enumerators were required to note the administrative counties of their districts on a new box in the top left-hand corner of the CEBs. In London particularly, where the London County Council had been newly created, the recent changes posed increasing challenges for local enumerators. The rapid growth of the population in the areas near the boundary changes in Walthamstow, for example, led to confusion over the edges of the district.

The census administrators, including the local government boards, wished to keep the enumeration districts in line with the previous census. As this did not take into account the larger populations and greater number of houses in some districts, some enumerators had more households to enumerate than others. The pattern of the census was similar to that of earlier years, with enumerators handing out schedules and collecting the following day. All schedules were due for collection by Tuesday, 7 April.

The Census Act of 1890 (53 & 54 Vict., c. 61) was passed on 18 August 1890. For this assessment, the census office was based in an iron building 'erected on a vacant plot of ground in Charles-street, opposite the offices of the Local Government Board'.[7] Sir Brydges Henniker and Dr William Ogle were supported in the running of the census by the secretary, Noel A. Humphreys, who had previously worked at the GRO, as well as 150 clerks. New personnel were recruited in 1891 since many of the previous administrators had retired.

In this year, Registrar General Brydges Henniker introduced new columns to the household schedule for number of rooms (if under five) and employment status. However, it was at the insistence of the social statistician, Charles Booth, and the leading economist, Professor Alfred Marshall – members of the 1890 Treasury Committee on the Census and critics of the GRO – that the employment changes were made. In 1884, Booth had looked extensively at census reports as part of his work in helping with the allocation of the Lord Mayor of London's relief fund. He found the returns to be inadequate for creating poverty statistics. On 18 May 1886, he read his report into the 'Occupations of the People of the United Kingdom, 1801–1881' before the Statistical Society.[8] In this, Booth highlighted the flaws in the current classification of occupations as used in the census reports. Although previous censuses had asked that masters were recorded in order to distinguish them from their employees, this was often ignored. There is evidence from those censuses that some farmers, managers, publicans, shopkeepers and so on did describe themselves as 'master' and did give the number of employees. Yet the practice was not widely adopted. Occupational statistics could be improved, Booth believed, with the insertion of this question. Henniker and Ogle disagreed, but were eventually overruled by the local government board.

For this census, women were allowed to become enumerators for the first time. *Jackson's Oxford Journal* of Saturday, 11 April 1891 (p.8)[9] wrote about the occasion with enthusiasm: 'Mr Draper had in his registrar's district the parishes of St. Giles, St. Clement, Cowley, Cowley St. John, St. John-the-Baptist, Headington, Marston, Elsfield, Wood Eaton, Stowood, Beckley, Horton-cum-Studley, Iffley, and Littlemore. He engaged the services of 28 enumerators, of whom several were women.'

Although the census allowed female enumerators, the forms still contained a printed 'Mr' after the 'Name of Enumerator'. Where women were enumerating, such as Bessie Cripps in district 21 of St Giles, Oxfordshire, the 'Mr' had to be corrected by hand to 'Miss' or 'Mrs'. Despite the newspaper's claims that there were 'several' women enumerators, a check of the CEBs on Ancestry reveals that there were only two in this area. The 27-year-old Miss Cripps may have acquired her position through family connection: the census of district 12 (ref. RG12/1165/89, p.28) reveals her father, Francis Cripps, was a solicitor and superintendent registrar of Headington.

Mrs Elizabeth Draper was an enumerator in district 17 of Cowley, and also in St Clement's district 17. Another Oxfordshire enumerator was John Draper. They would appear to be the John and Elizabeth Draper who were enumerated on the census at district 17 of Cowley, and 48-year-old John was employed as the registrar of births, deaths and marriages, relief officer, vaccination and school attendance officer and collector of guardians. This may explain how his wife, 44-year-old Elizabeth, acquired her position. From these examples, it does not appear that in 1891 women were employed as enumerators on the same terms as men.

Bearing in mind that one of John Draper's many roles was officer of school attendance, it is probable that the following instance refers to his wife:

> Among the incidents in the work may be mentioned the case of a lady enumerator who was suspected of being the bearer of School Board summonses, and who had the front door loudly slammed in her face, while to another was attributed the belief that she was on the look out for defaulters in the matter of dog licences.

The census day, 5 April 1891, fell in the Easter vacation of many schools and universities. Easter Sunday fell on 30 March, just one week before census night. Thus some pupils and students were away from home or school and appear on the census in unexpected locations. The statistics for certain districts, such as the university city of Oxford, were affected by this.

In Eastern Europe, anti-Jewish pogroms had been taking place since the assassination of Tsar Alexander II of Russia in March 1881. Many sought sanctuary from persecution and life in ghettos by fleeing to Britain, or rested there en route to the United States. At the end of the century, Jews formed the 'majority of alien immigrants' to Britain.[10] This increased immigration of mainly Yiddish and German speakers created a new challenge for census administrators. Enumerators in areas of high Jewish population in the East End of London were given crib sheets in Yiddish and German to hand out to householders, along with the English household schedules. The householders would use the crib to help them complete the form in English. However, inevitable confusion arose and, as a result, many recent Jewish immigrants were not correctly enumerated, and thus can be difficult to find on the census, or were not enumerated at all.

What Details are Included?

The population continued to climb, with the total this year believed to be 33,015,701. The population of England and Wales was 29,001,018.[11]

On 5 April 1891, the employment status of those who gave their occupations was noted. Also related to employment, in the occupation column the word 'rank' was removed. This perhaps reflected the more egalitarian Britain that Salisbury sought to create. The new question asked whether an inhabitant was an employer, employed or neither.

Another new question asked for the number of rooms occupied, if less than five:

- ROAD, STREET, &c. and No. or NAME of HOUSE
- HOUSES Inhabited
  Uninhabited
- Number of rooms occupied if less than five
- NAME and Surname of each Person
- RELATION to Head of Family
- CONDITION as to Marriage
- AGE last Birthday of
- Profession, or OCCUPATION
- Employer
- Employed
- Neither Employer nor Employed
- WHERE BORN
- If (1) Deaf-and-Dumb, (2) Blind, (3) Lunatic, Imbecile or Idiot
- Language Spoken (Wales).

The enumerators were instructed that each individual's middle initial 'must be inserted'.

The enumerators' books had sections for administrative county, civil parish, municipal borough, municipal ward, urban sanitary district, town or village or hamlet, rural sanitary district, parliamentary borough or division, and ecclesiastical parish or district. In this year, the description of the enumeration district given on the first page of the CEB was separated into the boundary and the area within.

The summary tables in the enumerators' books included the following:

- Number of schedules, houses (inhabited, uninhabited, being built), tenements of less than five rooms, and males and females in each named civil parish or township, or parts thereof
- As above for other administrative areas
- As above but for each page of the nominal returns.

Some alterations were made to the enumeration of ships. Enumerators would deliver the schedules to British, foreign or colonial ships employed in the coastal trade of the United Kingdom, which were anchored in port anytime between 30 March and 5 April. Others arriving between 6 April and 30 June were also enumerated. In this year, to simplify enumeration, fishing boats were enumerated in the same way as larger ships. No separate enumeration was made for members of the armed forces.

The Scottish census return became even more detailed, with the addition of a language column for those who spoke Scots-Gaelic:

The undermentioned Houses are situate within the Boundaries of the Civil Parish of/Quoad Sacra Parish of/School Board District of/Parliamentary Burgh of/Parliamentary Division of/Royal Burgh of/Municipal Burgh of/Police Burgh of/Burgh Ward of/Town of/Village of/Hamlet of/Island of

- ROAD, STREET, &c., and No or NAME of HOUSE
- HOUSES Inhabited
  Uninhabited (U) or Building (B)
- NAME and Surname of each Person
- RELATION to Head of Family
- CONDITION as to Marriage
- AGE (Last Birthday) of
  Males
  Females
- PROFESSION, or OCCUPATION
  Employer
  Employed
  Neither Employer nor Employed, but working on own account
- WHERE BORN
- GAELIC or G. & E.
- Whether 1. Deaf and Dumb. 2. Blind. 3. Lunatic, Imbecile, or Idiot.
- Rooms with One or more Windows.

Finding Aids

Besides the usual finding aids at TNA and local record offices, local groups have produced books, CD-ROMs and websites with name indexes for this census.

The 1891 'London Census Transcription' was created in 2003 as part of a Jack the Ripper project. The website at **www.census1891.com** contains name and street indexes and links to a 'Jack the Ripper map of Spitalfields & Whitechapel 1888'.

The Haverhill Family History Group has an online 1891 census index for a number of parishes in Suffolk. These can be searched at **www.haverhill-uk.com/genealogy/census/index.shtml**.

The census of St Veryan in Devon this year is at **http://freepages.rootsweb.com/~dtrounce/genealogy/veryanlists6.html**.

The Cornwall Online Census Project web page for 1891 is at **https://sites.rootsweb.com/~kayhin/cocp_1891.html**.

Online Resources

Ancestry allows searches of the 1891 census with the same options as for 1881, but without the free transcriptions. These records are online in partnership with The National Archives, who first digitized the record at **www.nationalarchives.gov.uk/census** in December 2004. The Ancestry database is most useful in identifying female enumerators as it includes digitized scans of the front pages of the CEBs.

MyHeritage offers a similar search to that of censuses in previous years: name, birth year and place, residence and keywords, with advanced options of birth date, relatives and image.

TheGenealogist has a page of statistics relating to each county for this census. The page for Radnorshire in Wales, for example, at **https://www.thegenealogist.co.uk/census/1891/radnorshire/** reveals that the most common surname in the county was Jones, the most common forename was Mary, and the top five occupations were scholar, farmer, farm servant, agricultural labourer and farmer's son, indicating the agrarian nature of the county.

Findmypast again offers searches by person or address. There is no free transcription.

FamilySearch's collection of 1891 census data includes 31,782,845 records, which is very good coverage. The collection can be searched directly at **www.familysearch.org/search/collection/1865747**. The transcription includes name, gender, age, relationship to head of household, birthplace, record type, registration district, sub-district, ecclesiastical parish, civil parish and county. The images can be viewed directly via Findmypast, although subscription fees apply there.

ScotlandsPeople provides full transcriptions and digital images of the Scottish census.

Scottish Census 1891 (Glasgow Royal Infirmary Ref. 644/03 120/03 017). (Reproduced with the kind permission of the Registrar General for Scotland)

Free Resources

The indexes and transcriptions at FamilySearch are free.

The FreeCen website provides links to transcriptions of census data for some parishes in the following counties:

Bedfordshire	Flintshire	Northamptonshire
Berkshire	Glamorgan	Nottinghamshire
Buckinghamshire	Gloucestershire	Oxfordshire
Caernarvonshire	Hampshire	Rutland
Caithness	Hertfordshire	Shropshire
Cambridgeshire	Huntingdonshire	Suffolk
Channel Islands	Kent	Somerset
Cheshire	Lancashire	Surrey
Cornwall	Leicestershire	Sussex
Derbyshire	Lincolnshire	Staffordshire
Denbighshire	London	Warwickshire
Devon	Middlesex	Wiltshire
Dorset	Norfolk	Worcestershire
County Durham	North Riding of	West Riding of
Essex	Yorkshire	Yorkshire

Problems

The missing parts of the 1891 census, as identified via TNA's Discovery catalogue using the keywords 'missing' or 'wanting', and the reference for this census, RG 12, reveals sixty-four unavailable pieces. These include:

- Victoria Hospital for Children, Chelsea, London
- Albert Industrial School, Birkenhead, Cheshire
- Monmouthshire Reformatory for Boys, Mamhilad, Monmouthshire
- Persons on a variety of vessels in parts of London, Kent, Devon, Staffordshire, Lincolnshire, Leicestershire, Lancashire, Somerset, County Durham, Selkirkshire, Glamorganshire and Montgomeryshire
- Compton Wyniates, Warwickshire.

The high number of persons missing from vessels may explain absences of merchant seamen, fishermen or canal boat ancestors in 1891.

How to Use the Census Effectively

The question of employment status did not only annoy Henniker and Ogle: many householders were reluctant to complete this question, or to give accurate answers. The accuracy of the answers is questionable on a number of fronts. Firstly, women who worked with their husbands were classed as 'employed' rather than 'on own account' or an 'employer'. However, this gives a false impression of the roles of many women within family businesses. In some cases, women were the main proprietors or managers of the commercial affairs.

Secondly, just as employers on previous censuses had neglected to describe themselves as 'master' or to include the number of their employees, so in 1891 the employment columns were often left blank. Those working in industrial occupations were asked to mark their column with a cross, but this, too, was sometimes ignored.[12]

Thirdly, as was the case with previous censuses, householders were confused by what was required of them, and marked the wrong column.

Family historians should be wary of the evidence provided by this column and seek to support it with occupational details from other sources, such as GRO certificates, apprentice records, trade directories or pensions.

Taking it Further

The number of rooms given on this census can provide useful detail from a social history perspective and also for those researching the history of houses. This can be taken further by examining rate books and property records, available at local record offices. Some details on the rooms in houses may even be found in legal records such as wills, or personal records such as letters, diaries or memoirs.

The chief problem with the use of the word 'room' in this census is that enumerators and householders were given no definition of what this should include. Thus, it is possible that some householders included the lobby, scullery or shop room that would be excluded from future censuses. This complicates research into homes. Those householders who left the column blank, suggesting a residence of more than five rooms, may have been giving a false impression as to how large their homes really were. A useful approach to this evidence, therefore, is to try to identify homes of similar sizes. Where a row of terraces have been built of exactly the same proportion, perhaps as identified in local government records, the numbers of rooms given for each can be compared and the accurate number identified.

Unique Features of the Non-English Censuses

In Scotland, the 1891 census asked for the number of rooms with one or more windows, contrasting with the English and Welsh question about five rooms or less. Another variation on the Scottish census was the question as to whether the members of the household spoke Gaelic, or Gaelic and English ('G. & E.').

Residents of Wales and Monmouthshire received a separate schedule from those in England. The Welsh schedule had an extra column headed 'Language Spoken'. Here, occupants were expected to record whether they spoke 'English', 'Welsh' or 'Both'. The census report revealed that 759,416 spoke only English, 508,036 spoke only Welsh, with 402,253 able to speak both.[13]

In the last chapter, the example of the Evans family in Henllan, Denbighshire revealed that they were Welsh-speaking. The fact that the householder required a Welsh schedule for the census of 1881 suggests that no one in the family could read English. In 1891, this family was still residing at 14 School Street (ref. RG12/4630/5, p.4) but no longer needed a Welsh schedule as shown by the absence of the 'W' in the first column. Both Edward Evans and his wife, Eunice, were recorded as speaking Welsh only. The only other occupant of the address on this census was their 23-year-old daughter, Margaret Ethel Evans, who was recorded as being able to speak both English and Welsh. This information fits with the assumption from the previous census, excepting Margaret Ethel's ability to speak English. However, as she was a 13-year-old scholar in 1881, it

1891 Census showing Welsh Speakers (Ref. RG12/4567/11 p.15). (© Crown Copyright Images reproduced by courtesy of The National Archives, London, England. www.NationalArchives.gov.uk & www.TheGenealogist.co.uk)

is possible that her parents were wary of relying on her interpretation of the English schedule.

Welsh nationalism was growing at the end of the nineteenth century. Henniker even highlighted this in the general report[14] of 1891 by suggesting that the number of Welsh speakers was greater as a result of nationalism. This may ignore the fact that many enumerators and householders were unsure how to answer the question, and whether it referred to all languages a person was able to speak, the main language used, or simply that used at work. Thus family historians should not rely solely on the marks in these columns to discover their Welsh ancestors' language habits or abilities.

Again, a religious census was taken only in Ireland. Although this remained optional, the vast majority of households continued to return the details of their religious profession. The census continued to be enumerated by the constabulary, who were known in this context as 'trained collectors of the statistical'.

The Scottish and Irish censuses were overseen by the respective Registrars General: Stair Agnew and Dr Thomas Grimshaw. Reports were created separately.

Summary

The 1891 census marked a major change for census-taking, the greatest since 1851, not least in response to local government changes and the demands of social scientists. The two most significant changes to the household schedule that year were the introduction of the question on rooms to the English and Welsh censuses, and the employment question for all. Employment marked a change in priority for census administrators and politicians, away from medical statistics to issues of working-class reform through the franchise and education. However, this innovation also highlighted the tensions between the GRO and those involved in local and national government and their advisory committees. The GRO's power over the census was proved to be weak, and Henniker was shown little respect in his position as Registrar General by others in government.

Chapter 9

1901: THE CENTENARY OF CENSUS-TAKING IN ENGLAND, SCOTLAND AND WALES

KEY EVENTS OF 1891–1901

- 1892: William Gladstone succeeds Lord Salisbury as prime minister
- 1893: Dr John Tatham becomes superintendent of statistics at the GRO
- 1895: Salisbury regains the office of prime minister
- 1899–1902: Second Boer War
- 1900: Reginald McLeod is appointed Registrar General
- 1901: Death of Queen Victoria at Osborne House on the Isle of Wight. Her eldest son, Albert, becomes King Edward VII of the United Kingdom and the British Dominions, and Emperor of India, heralding the new Edwardian age.

The 1896 Quinquennial Census

On the night of 29 March 1896, a census of the County of London was taken by the local government and taxation committee of the London County Council under the Equalization of Rates Act 1894. The manner of census-taking was the same as that of the decennial censuses, with papers delivered in the week leading up to the census night and collected on the following Monday. Schedules were handed out to those on vessels as well as in buildings. Strict instructions were given that 'no person dying before midnight, and no child born after midnight, is to be enumerated'.[1]

Papers relating to this census and to the proposed censuses of 1906 and 1916 are held at The National Archives in reference RG 19/42. However, the enumerators' books, including the details of name, sex and relationship to head of household, are believed not to have survived. A statistical return of the census is held at the London Metropolitan Archives in the series SC/PPS/063, 'London County Council Publications: Official Publications: Numbered Series'. The *Return of population enumerated in Civil Parishes in Administrative county of London, Mar. 1896, pursuant to Section 3 of London (Equalisation of Rates) Act, 1894* can be read online at the HISTPOP website.

Historical Context

Census enumerators delivering household schedules in the week leading up to Sunday, 31 March had to battle against fierce gales in harsh, cold weather. Snow and soft hail fell over the entire British Isles, and the east coast was subject to thunderstorms on Thursday the 28th. The gales caused havoc around the coast, with the loss of several lives from the steamship *Paris* off Northumberland on the 29th.

By March 1901, Britain had been involved in the Second Boer War in South Africa for two years. Throughout the conflict, the contemporary newspapers, music hall songs and popular literature kept the British public informed, and often entertained, by the exploits of the imperial forces and their leaders. Journalists, such as the young Winston Churchill of the *Morning Post* and his aunt, Sarah Wilson of the *Daily Mail*, made heroes of the empire out of the besieged forces of Mafeking and their leader Colonel (later Lord) Baden Powell, when they were relieved in May 1900. Parties and celebrations broke out across the nation, and 18 May 1900 became known as 'Mafeking Night'. Beyond the patriotism and media glorification, the war was a strain on British financial and military resources. The fighting would last another year after census night, until 31 May 1902, creating around 59,000 British casualties. At least half of these are believed to have died from illness relating to poor sanitary conditions. Their names, and those of some of the men who served in the war, can be found online in the Second Anglo-Boer War register at Findmypast.

The preliminary report of the 1901 census shows that the population of England and Wales numbered 32,526,075, of which 15,721,728 were male and 16,804,347 were female. In London, the largest city in Britain, the population enumerated was 4,536,063. The report states this was an increase from the 1891 census of 7.3 per cent, a far smaller percentage than the increase in London's population in previous years. The greatest increase in London's population between the decennial censuses, according to this document, had been between 1841 and 1851, when the city grew by 21.2 per cent, and between 1811 and 1821 the population had grown by 21.1 per cent.[2]

The census process was also going through a period of renewal. Sir Brydges Henniker retired in 1900 and was replaced by Reginald McLeod (1847–1935) as Registrar General.[3] Henniker's rule at the GRO was unpopular with his employees, and others who worked with him, for being unambitious and for deferring constantly to the local government board. Nevertheless, family historians have reason to be grateful to him. In 1891, Henniker challenged the LGB when it wanted to destroy the 1851 and 1861 CEBs (then housed in Victoria Tower in the Houses of Parliament). Instead, Henniker turned to experts from the Public Record Office, who agreed that the CEBs should remain. Without Henniker, therefore, the research of today's family historians would be far more difficult.

Another change was that Dr William Ogle retired from his post as Superintendent of Statistics at the GRO in 1893. He was replaced by Dr John Tatham (1844–1924), a qualified physician and experienced medical statistician.

The Census Act of 1900 (Act 63 & 64 Vict., c. 4) was passed on 27 March that year.

Women's roles as enumerators had been much commented on in 1891. In 1901 they were employed, for the first time, as temporary clerks in the census office, now situated in Millbank near the Houses of Parliament. These women proved their worth and many of them would later be employed by McLeod as full-time staff of the GRO. In 1901, they were some of the 31.6 per cent of females over the age of 10 recorded on the census as being in paid employment.

As in 1891, the female clerks that were employed often had a prior connection to the census. For example, 28-year-old Indian-born Charlotte Benstead, who was described in the CEB for Brook Street, Southwark as working as a 'Forewoman at Census Office', was living with her 61-year-old father, Henry Benstead, who worked as an 'Office keeper at Census Office' (ref. RG13/369/111, p.38).

Reginald McLeod oversaw the census process in 1901, but after 1902 when he moved to Scotland as Permanent Under Secretary, a new Registrar General was appointed who would supervise the preparation of the report. This new Registrar General was William Cospatrick Dunbar (1844–1931). The census reports, published under Dunbar in 1902, were arranged by county in fifty-three separate volumes. Previous reports had presented the data on housing, population and so on in one volume.

What Details are Included?

The enumerators' books in England, Wales and the islands asked for administrative county, civil parish, ecclesiastical parish, county borough/municipal borough/urban district, ward of municipal borough or of urban district, rural district, parliamentary borough or division, and town or village or hamlet.

The information requested on the schedules was similar to that of 1891, and included the column for 'Number of Rooms occupied if less than five'. There were a few small changes in 1901. For example, the number of the house was requested officially (previously any inclusion of numbers was optional). More information was also requested in the 'Inhabited' section, which now asked whether a dwelling was inhabited, in occupation, not in occupation, or building.

The employment question was changed to one column, but with an extra question asking if inhabitants worked from home. In this column, householders were expected to write whether each working person was an 'employer', 'worker' or working on 'own account'. This change is believed to have been made as a result of demands from the Home Office, with regard to potential legislation for regulating the 'sweated trades'.[4]

The disability column for this year was amended to include four options: 'deaf and dumb', 'blind', 'lunatic' and 'imbecile or feeble-minded'.

The summary tables in the enumerators' books included the following:

- Number of schedules, houses (inhabited, uninhabited, being built), tenements of less than five rooms, and males and females in each named civil parish or township, or parts thereof
- As above for other administrative areas
- As above but for each page of the nominal returns.

The Scottish census included the changes made in the English and Welsh census, but retained the column asking for number of rooms with one or more windows.

Civil Parish of/Parish Ward of/Ecclesiastical Parish of/Quoad Sacra Parish of/School Board District of/Parliamentary Division of/Royal Burgh of/Municipal Burgh of/Police Burgh of/Burgh Ward of/Town of/Island of

- NO. of Schedule
- ROAD, street, &c., and No. or NAME of HOUSE

- HOUSES Inhabited
  Uninhabited (U) or Building (B)
- NAME and Surname of each Person
- RELATION to Head of Family
- CONDITION as to Marriage
- AGE (last Birthday)
  Males
  Females
- PROFESSION, or OCCUPATION
- Employer, Worker or on own Account
- If Working at Home
- WHERE BORN
- GAELIC or G. & E.
- Whether 1. Deaf and Dumb. 2. Blind. 3. Lunatic. 4. Imbecile, feeble- minded
- Rooms with One or more Windows.

The Census of Ireland, 1901, form A: 'RETURN of the MEMBERS of this FAMILY and their VISITORS, BOARDERS, SERVANTS, &c., who slept or abode in this House on the night of SUNDAY, the 31st of MARCH, 1901' included detailed instructions on the form. They were:

- Number (of Schedule)
- NAME and SURNAME – Christian Name/Surname
- No persons ABSENT on the night of Sunday, March 31st, to be entered here: EXCEPT those (not enumerated elsewhere) who may be out at WORK or TRAVELLING, &c., during that Night, and who RETURN HOME ON MONDAY, APRIL 1st./Subject to the above instruction, the Name of the Head of the Family should be written first: then the names of his Wife, Children, and other Relatives: then those of Visitors, Boarders, Servants, &c.
- RELATION to Head of Family
  State whether 'Head of Family' or 'Wife', 'son', 'daughter', or other relative : 'visitor', 'boarder', 'servant', &c.
- RELIGIOUS PROFESSION
  State here the particular Religion, or Religious Denomination, to which each person belongs (Members of Protestant Denominations are requested not to describe themselves by the vague term 'Protestant', but to enter the name of the Particular church, Denomination, or Body, to which they belong.)

- EDUCATION
  State here whether he or she can 'Read and Write', can 'Read' only, or 'Cannot Read'
- AGE
  Years on last Birthday / Months for Infants under One Year
- SEX
  Write 'M' for Males and 'F' for Females
- RANK, PROFESSION, OR OCCUPATION
  State the Particular Rank, Profession, Trade, or other Employment of each person. Children or young persons attending a School, or receiving regular instruction at home, should be returned as *Scholars*. [Before filling this column you are requested to read the Instructions on the other side.]
- MARRIAGE
  Whether 'Married', 'Widower', 'Widow', or 'Not Married'
- WHERE BORN
  If in Ireland, state in which County or City: if elsewhere, state the name of the Country
- IRISH LANGUAGE
  Write the word 'Irish' in this column opposite the name of each person who speaks Irish *only*, and the words 'Irish & English' opposite the names of those who can speak both languages. In other cases no entry should be made in this column
- If Deaf and Dumb; Dumb only; blind; Imbecile or Idiot; or Lunatic
  Write the respective infirmities opposite the name of the afflicted person.

The returns are arranged by townland or, in urban areas, by street.

In Ireland, those living outside domestic dwellings were enumerated on different forms from Form A described above. These forms were as follows:

- B3 shipping returns
- C sick at home
- D lunatics and idiots at home
- E workhouses
- F hospitals
- G academic bodies
- H barracks
- I asylums
- K prisons.

Finding Aids

The *Survey Gazetteer of the British Isles* includes a list of place names in the 1901 census.

Street indexes are held at The National Archives and relevant local record offices.

An index to institutions that were enumerated separately from ordinary households in the 1901 census can be explored at **http:// jefferyknaggs.com/Instuts.html**.

Online Resources

The household returns and related records for the 1901 Census of Ireland are the earliest to survive (mostly) in full. They are held at the National Archives of Ireland. The returns for all thirty-two counties have been digitized in partnership with Library and Archives Canada. Searches, transcriptions and original images are all free at the census website **www.census.nationalarchives.ie**. Some parts are missing. These pieces were either never in the custody of the NAI or were not previously microfilmed and are now in the process of being digitized.

This website is extremely useful for family historians. It can be searched by name, religion, occupation, relationship to head of the family, literacy status, county or country of origin, Irish-language ability and specified illnesses. Not only is all the information free, but users can also access transcriptions as well as images of the household returns, enumerators' abstracts, house and building returns, and out-office and farmstead returns.

In the case of institutions, often only the initials rather than the full names of inhabitants are recorded. Thus an ancestor who was in the police, the services or who was mentally ill may need to be identified through other historical records.

This example shows the transcription page from the website for Mary Farrell, a 51-year-old lodger residing at 7.2 Evelyn Gardens in Clifton Ward, Belfast. Her religion is given as Church of Ireland. Lower down the page to the left are the options for viewing images. Once clicked, these open up PDF images of the original returns. At the top of the screen are options for browsing the census, searching and tips on 'How to Search' effectively. There is also a digital exhibition of 'Early 20th century Ireland', which provides useful socio-historical background to the lives being led there at this time.

The original return reveals even more detail. Mary Farrell can read and write, and receives an 'Income from dividends'. She is 'Not married' and she was born in County Down. In the top right-hand corner of the

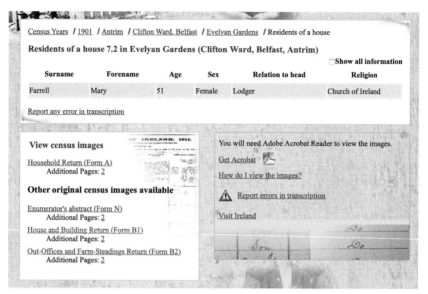

1901 Census Transcription for the entry of Mary Farrell as shown on the National Archives of Ireland's census website.

schedule is the 'No. on Form B.' – in this case, it is 7. This requires a return to the website transcription page and a click on Form B1. On this PDF page, we need to look at number 7 in the schedule. This is the house where Mary Farrell lives. This provides detailed information on

1901 Irish Census entry showing Mary Farrell.

the building, including the materials out of which the walls and roof are built. The number of rooms is stated, although these are grouped into the following number of rooms: 1, 2–4, 5–6, 7–9, 10–12, 12 or more. Mary Farrell's property has 10–12 rooms, although this form reveals that she shares it with another household, headed by Alexander Frew. Her property has twelve windows in the front of the house. However, while Alexander Frew's family of two occupies nine rooms, Mary Farrell only occupies two. There is an option to give the name of the landowner, which is useful if your ancestors were tenant farmers. In Mary Farrell's case no landowner is named. Form N is the enumerator's abstract and gives an overview of the street. County Down is now part of Northern Ireland, and it is no surprise that of thirty-eight people enumerated, only two are Roman Catholic. The twenty-six Protestant residents comprise members of the Church of Ireland, Presbyterians, one Independent, Methodists, 'other Protestants' and Quakers.

When searching for occupations, use the master search on TheGenealogist as this allows a surname or forename plus keyword search (using the 'Find a Person within Census' option). The search is more effective if a specific census year is identified. The keyword could be a place or occupation or other term relevant to the search.

The census records on Ancestry can be more difficult to search for occupations, although Scottish data is more detailed than that of England, Wales, the Isle of Man and the Channel Islands. For example, a search of the 1901 census for the keyword 'laundress' gives the following results:

Scotland	10,251
England	190
Isle of Man	7
Wales	7
Channel Islands	1

There were far more laundresses in England than 190. A search of the 1901 census on Findmypast for persons with occupation 'laundress' in London alone reveals 588. However, even this is not accurate as it omits my second great-grand-aunt, Millie Barnes, who was enumerated on the border of Stoke Newington and Islington, north London (ref. RG13/197/109, p.28). This highlights the errors that are present in the transcriptions for this and other censuses. As they vary between websites, it is worth trying to find your ancestor with different census providers. Using surname only or address options can help you locate an ancestor where the website persists in not identifying them.

1901 Scottish Census entry (Avondale Lanarkshire Ref. 621/00 009/00 002). (Reproduced with the kind permission of the Registrar General for Scotland)

Scottish census transcripts and images can be explored in full at ScotlandsPeople. The 1901 Scottish census was placed online in January 2002, following the release of the English and Welsh census.

Scottish census transcriptions can be found at Ancestry, GenesReunited and Findmypast.

The original 1901 census website, **www.1901censusonline.com**, launched with great interest in January 2002. The site proved so popular on its first day that it crashed. More than 1.2 million people had tried to find family or house history information. The site is free to search by person, place, institution, vessel or reference number. It gives free access to a brief transcription, but requires payment to access full transcriptions and images. The shorter transcription includes name, age, where born, administrative county, civil parish and occupation. The brief transcription for the address search reveals address, how occupied, administrative county, civil parish, ecclesiastical parish, parliamentary borough, municipal borough and municipal ward.

The 1901 census online website has since been absorbed into the Findmypast database.

Free Resources

The most significant free resource for the 1901 census is that of the Irish census.

The indexes on Ancestry and Findmypast are free. FamilySearch includes transcriptions of this census for England and Wales, and for Scotland.

The FreeCen website does not cover the 1901 census.

Searches for those aboard Royal Navy vessels can be found for free at **http://jefferyknaggs.com/RNShips.html**.

Problems

There are fewer known missing pieces of the 1901 census than for previous years. Those that are known include some enumeration books for areas within the sub-district of Deal in Kent, which are recorded as being 'missing at transfer'.

Described as 'wanting' in The National Archives' Discovery catalogue is part of the registration sub-district of St Giles North and Bloomsbury and St Giles South, both in London.

Known to be missing are numbers 1–14 Doughty Mews in Holborn, St Pancras, London.

The reference for this census is RG 13. Royal Navy ships at sea or in ports should be found in RG13 / 5325-5335, but several are missing. A list of those either not recorded or that did not survive can be seen at **http://jefferyknaggs.com/RNShips.html**.

How to Use the Census Effectively

The 1901 houses column was divided into four parts: inhabited houses, uninhabited houses, uninhabited houses which were not usually in occupation and those which were being built. For this census, the number of rooms question was clarified: a room was defined as including the kitchen, but not any scullery, landing, lobby, closet, bathroom, warehouse, office or shop.

The National Archives hosts a digital exhibition on housing in 1901 at **www.nationalarchives.gov.uk/pathways/census/living/live/home.htm**.

Taking it Further

Charles Booth (1840–1916), the pioneering sociologist and philanthropist whose demands for the 1891 census had frustrated Sir Brydges Henniker, had spent the following decade furthering his investigations into London's poor. This involved exploring all streets in London, and occasionally lodging with working-class families.[5] His work was expanded into the nine-volume *Life and Labour of the People in London* (1892–97).

As part of the investigation, Booth and his team produced coloured maps of London. These 'poverty maps' – *Maps Descriptive of London Poverty, 1898–9* – provide a useful insight into London streets and residents of 1901. The streets on the map were coloured to represent the social class of those who lived there. Booth categorized the classes into seven distinct groups, ranging from the lowest, vicious and semi-criminal class (whose homes were coloured black) to the wealthy upper-middle and upper classes (yellow on the map).

The survey into life and labour in London was begun in 1886 and came to an end in 1903. The maps and other material from the Booth collections of the archive division of the library of the London School of Economic and Political Science and the Senate House Library can be found at the Charles Booth Online Archive: **http://booth.lse.ac.uk**.

The maps can be searched by streets, postcodes and wards in 2000, and landmarks and parishes in 1898. This can be problematic for a family historian who is researching ancestors on a street that was demolished or altered before 2000. In this case, a nearby existing street can be found and the neighbourhood explored through any notebook entry and on the corresponding maps. Otherwise, the parishes can be browsed.

As an example, Millie Barnes was living and running a laundry in Boleyn Road. Booth records in his notebook that nearby Sultan Place is 'also poor, drunken costers. The Lord Clyde Coffee House at the corner has been a noted brothel for years.'[6] Boleyn Road itself he describes as '2 storied & purple in character, street run up hill to the north … here rather poorer [than Wolsey Grove]. 2 stories on west side. Dr. Ridge's food factory on the East Side.'

In 1901, the now 61-year-old Booth appears on the census at his country home of Grace Dieu Manor in Leicestershire. He is described simply as 'Ship Owner', his chief occupation and source of income during the years he spent investigating London's poor (ref. RG13/109/2975/37 p.17).

Unique Features of the Non-English Censuses

In Wales and Monmouthshire, a column was again included for 'Language Spoken'. This column was added to the census of the Isle of Man. In this case, residents needed to respond with whether they spoke Manx, English or both. The only exemptions from these columns should have been children under 3 years old. The Irish census included an 'Irish Language' column, which allowed for options of speaking Irish only, or Irish and English.

The most significant difference between the Irish census and that of the others is the inclusion of 'Religious Profession' and 'Education' (or the ability to read and write, read only or illiterate). Illiterate persons marked their names with an X in front of the enumerator. Both of these columns provide details that can lead to other sources. Use the religious profession and the address of your ancestor to identify the nearest respective church or chapel. Surviving records of this institution can then be explored in the relevant archive. Where an ancestor is revealed as illiterate, care should be taken over any details they have revealed. The spelling of the surname, for example, may be subject to variation, and there may even be uncertainty about the age. An ancestor who reveals an ability to read and write, along with an ability to speak English, is likely to have been educated at school or with a private tutor. Thus, it would be worth consulting surviving local school records or searching further to find a boarding school or higher academic institution that he or she may have attended.

The website **https://www.nifhs.org/resources/miscellaneous-records/census-strays/** can help find ancestors who have moved away from their birthplace. The Leitrim-Roscommon 1901 Census Home Page **www.leitrim-roscommon.com/1901census** has 1901 census entries for the counties of Galway, Leitrim, Mayo, Roscommon, Sligo, Wexford and Westmeath. When searching the Irish census, it is useful to be aware of the Irish language and to try variants of surnames beginning with O and Mc/Mac.

The Scottish census was overseen for the third time by the recently knighted Registrar General, Sir Stair Agnew.

In Ireland, the Registrar General Dr Thomas Grimshaw died on 23 January 1900. He was succeeded by the Right Honourable Sir Robert Edwin Matheson (1845–1926).

Summary

By 1901, the census across Britain and Ireland was taken efficiently and was the most detailed it had ever been. The Irish census was especially detailed, and family historians are fortunate in that the records for this year not only survived but have been fully digitized on a searchable free website. However, there are limitations to the English and Welsh transcription online and perseverance is needed to identify all ancestors. Although some useful language details are provided, not all languages spoken are included in this census. We are unaware, for example, of the ability of those who spoke Yiddish, German, Russian, other European languages or Indian languages. We also do not know who in Ireland could not speak Irish. With new Registrars General in place in England, Scotland and Ireland further changes would be made, leading to the creation, in the 1911 census, of one of the most useful documents for British and Irish family, social and local history research.

Chapter 10

1911: THE FERTILITY CENSUS

Historical Context

KEY EVENTS OF 1901–1911
- 1906: Liberal landslide victory at the General Election
- 1907: Eugenics Society founded
- 1908: London hosts the Olympic Games
- 1908–19: Herbert Henry (H.H.) Asquith serves as prime minister and leader of the Liberal Party
- 1909: Lloyd George's 'People's Budget'
- 1909: Majority and Minority Reports of the Royal Commission on the Poor Laws and Relief of Distress
- 1909: Bernard Mallett is appointed Registrar General
- 1909: Thomas Henry Craig Stevenson is appointed Superintendent of Statistics
- 1909: James Patten McDougall is appointed Registrar General of Scotland
- 1909: Sir William John Thompson is appointed Registrar General of Ireland
- 1910: Death of King Edward VII; his eldest son becomes King George V
- 1910: Two General Elections are held (January and December)
- 1911: Parliament Act; reduces power of the peers
- 1911: National Insurance Act
- 1911: Coronation of King George V.

The Census (Great Britain) Act of 1910 (10 Edw. VII, c. 27) legislated for the 1911 census, which would take place on Sunday, 2 April. The censuses of Scotland and Ireland also took place on this day. The census office for England, Wales and the 'Islands in the British Seas' remained behind the Tate Gallery in Millbank, in its brick and corrugated iron buildings. William Cospatrick Dunbar was a keen proponent of more frequent census enumeration, but his plans were not achieved and he resigned in 1909. Bernard Mallett (1859–1932) became the sixth Registrar General, remaining in position until 1920. He was knighted in 1916. A new Superintendent of Statistics, Thomas Henry Craig Stevenson (1870–1932), was appointed in 1909.

The Scottish census was also overseen by a new Registrar General, James Patten McDougall, who had been appointed in March 1909. He would be knighted in 1914. In 1911, the Scottish census-taking involved the sheriff of counties and the chief magistrates receiving the CEBs and then passing them on to McDougall. In England and Wales, in contrast, the CEBs were sent directly to the census office. McDougall's chief assistant in assessing the returns was the Superintendent of Statistics in Scotland, James C. Dunlop.

Over in Ireland, another Registrar General was appointed in 1909. Sir William John Thompson, a qualified physician, served in the role from 1909 to 1926. In 1911, complying with his position, he acted as the chairman of the Census Commission 1911. Once again, enumeration was undertaken by the police. Both the Scottish and Irish censuses were less demanding on their administrators than that of England and Wales as a result of their far smaller populations. In contrast to an estimated English and Welsh population in 1911 of 36,070,492, the preliminary report revealed an Irish population of 4,381,951 (later altered to 4,390,219), a decrease of 1.7 per cent from 1901.[1] The 1911 population of Scotland was 4,760,904.

During Edward's reign, concern among politicians, eugenicists and others grew over what was considered a high level of immigration, particularly from Eastern Europe. Disturbing as it would seem to most of us today, many of those involved with the census of 1911 were sympathetic to the theory of eugenics. Prime Minister Asquith's wife sat on a committee for legalizing eugenic sterilization, and the Registrar General, Bernard Mallett, would go on to be president of the Eugenics Society (founded in 1907 by Francis Galton).

Eugenics was a pseudo-science, developed by the proto-geneticist Francis Galton in 1883. The term, coined by Galton, derived from the Greek works for 'good' and 'origin'. A cousin of Charles Darwin, Galton was interested in theories of evolution that showed a removal of 'undesirables' from plant and animal species. Galton sought to extend these theories to the British population. The followers of eugenics, who included key social reformers, were keen to prevent or reduce the reproduction of the 'undesirable' or 'unfit'. Their definition included those who were poor, criminal, disabled or chronically ill. By 1911, eugenicists formed part of the 'National Efficiency' movement, influencing the movement for welfare reform. One of their chief concerns in the aftermath of the Second Boer War was the fitness of what was termed the 'Imperial Race' or 'Anglo-Saxons'. They, it was argued, must not be tainted by interbreeding with non-Britons.

This attitude was to influence the debate leading to the enforcement of the 1905 Aliens Act in 1906 by the Liberal Campbell-Bannerman government. This Act would restrict 'undesirable immigrants' who may make too high demands upon English welfare benefits. These 'undesirables' were essentially those immigrants who were sick and poor, and there followed a fierce political debate over immigration. *Hansard* (29.1.1902) reports a speech by the Conservative MP William Evans Gordon, who argued:

> Not a day passes by English families are ruthlessly turned out to make room for Foreign invaders.... Out they go to make room for Rumanians, Russians and Poles.... It is only a matter of time before the population becomes entirely foreign.... The rates are burdened with the education of thousands of children of foreign parents.... The working classes know that new buildings are erected not for them but for strangers from abroad.

Trade unions (such as the National Boiler Makers), socialists (like Ben Tillett) and the far-right British Brothers League shared politicians' concerns, all arguing for immigration controls. Many believed that Jews, who made up the majority of Eastern European immigrants in this period, were harmful to Britain, threatening national institutions and traditions.[2] Such attitudes were common across Europe at this time and would have devastating consequences in the following decades. A new column in the census reflected this national mood, asking for the nationality of those born outside the country in order to establish the exact size of the alleged threat. Within this column, in order to account for all immigrants, individuals were asked to clarify whether they were British by parentage or naturalization. The Scottish census report would reveal 6,102 Russians living there in 1911; other sizeable immigrant groups were 4,930 Poles, 4,594 Italians and 2,362 Germans.

The decade leading up to the 1911 census featured numerous investigations into the welfare of the poor. However, the political debate on welfare in England and Wales was dominated by the National

Insurance Act of 1911, which had been proposed in 1909's 'People's Budget' by David Lloyd George, the Chancellor of the Exchequer. This Act led to the introduction of a contributory medical and unemployment insurance for workers. The first part of the National Insurance scheme, which would come into effect in July 1912, ensured that medical benefits would be provided to workers (with earnings of less than £160/year) who paid a weekly contribution of 4d. Their employers would pay 3d and the government contributed 2d.

The second part insured against unemployment: employers would pay 2.5d per week, employees aged 16 to 70 paid 2.5d, and the government 3d. In return, unemployed workers would receive 7s per week for up to fifteen weeks a year. The figures were based on an unemployment rate of 4.6 per cent or less. If this figure rose, the national economy would be threatened. This political preoccupation with employment and, pointedly, numbers in unemployment led to the introduction of another new column in the census. This asked for the industry in which the population worked.

The National Insurance Act was not popular with everyone. Some of the loudest protests came from those who employed servants. Although the English and Welsh census would show that the number of servants had reduced from 1891, domestic service remained the largest occupational category with 1.3 million employed, followed by agriculture (1.2 million) and coal-mining (971,000). These figures were out of a total English and Welsh population of 36,003,276. The Scottish population was reported to be 4.75 million, with the highest number of male workers in iron and metal manufacture, followed by agriculture and coal-mining. As in England and Wales, the majority of female workers in Scotland were domestic servants.

Many workers wanted more independent lives and the census showed an increase in the numbers of clerks and shop workers, of both sexes. The summer was to see a period known as the 'Great Unrest', with strikes among dockers, railwaymen and miners. Some of those involved in the strikes would become involved in the incipient Labour Party.

The biggest change in the administration of the census was the introduction of tabulation. This was intended to simplify the census process. Tabulation, which was already well established in US census administration, replaced the copying of schedules into CEBs. Instead, the administrators used punch cards and machines to sort and count the papers. The main effect of this for today's family historians is that the copies of the English, Welsh and Irish censuses we see on our screens are scanned from the original schedules, rather than from the pages of the

CEBs. For this reason, we can see the original handwriting and signatures of our householder ancestors. This provides an opportunity to see an ancestor's signature and perhaps compare it with another elsewhere in case of uncertain identity. Unfortunately, the household schedules for Scotland have not survived, and only the enumerators' schedules can be viewed on ScotlandsPeople.

The year 1911 became known as the year of the fertility census. Mallett's preoccupation with eugenics influenced his decision to introduce to the household schedule questions about the total number of births of married women in their present marriage. This number was broken down into those still alive and those who had died, and so this was the first time that deceased members of the family were included in a census. Eugenicists had argued that the working classes were breeding more than the middle classes, leading to an inferior 'Imperial Race'.[3] The subsequent report, *Census of England and Wales, 1911, Vol. XII: Fertility of Marriage*, appeared to confirm the eugenicists' fears. It was revealed that the average family had 2.8 children, but this number increased among the working classes. For its report into fertility, the GRO divided society into five classes. These were based on the occupations of the heads of household.

Although the process of census administration had been simplified, the complete fertility report would only be produced in 1923. The amount of data produced by this census was far greater than in previous years and took longer to analyse. The reporting process would also be interrupted by the war of 1914–18.

In Wales, the Nonconformist movement grew stronger, and 1911 saw increasing demands for the disestablishment of the Anglican Church in Wales. This would eventually prove successful with the Welsh Church Act of 1914. In Wales, census enumerators continued to use both English and Welsh forms. Where schedules were completed in Welsh, entries are transcribed in that language. This should be borne in mind when searching for Welsh-speaking ancestors.

What Details are Included?

Those who were enumerated, in addition to details found on previous censuses, gave their nationality, the industry or service worked in, duration of current marriage and the number of children born to that marriage. They should also have numbered how many of those children were still living and how many had died. This can be a particularly useful column in identifying children who had been born and died between censuses. However, not all householders completed this correctly.

In 1911, for the first time, the census counted members of the armed forces stationed outside the British Isles and their family members individually. This is particularly useful for establishing whether military ancestors were living with wives and children at their garrisons or on ships. As Simon Fowler reveals:

> In January 1911 the War Office issued an Army Order directing local commanders to ensure that proper details of the men under their command were entered into special books…. Men's names, age, rank and place of birth were noted down. But native bearers, servants or civilian employees are not recorded. Neither were British officers serving in the Indian Army.[4]

Women and children were enumerated separately from their military husbands. Thus it is necessary to search for two separate census records. For women, details were given of the length of marriage, number of children and birthplaces. Separate census returns were made for members of the Royal Navy at sea. Search online using keyword 'military'.

The full list of questions on the English and Welsh censuses is as follows:

1. NAME AND SURNAME of every Person, whether Member of Family, Visitor, Boarder, or Servant, who (1) passed the night of Sunday, April 2nd, 1911, in this dwelling and was alive at midnight, or (2) arrived in this dwelling on the morning of Monday, April 3rd, not having been enumerated elsewhere.
2. RELATIONSHIP to Head of Family.
3. AGE (last Birthday) and SEX.
4. PARTICULARS as to MARRIAGE. Write 'Single', 'Married', 'Widower', or 'Widow', opposite the names of all persons aged 15 years and upwards. State, for each Married Woman entered on this schedule, the number of: Completed years the present Marriage has lasted / Children born alive to present Marriage / Total Children born Alive / Children still Living / Children who have Died.
5. PROFESSION or OCCUPATION of Persons aged ten years and upwards. Personal Occupation / Industry or Service with which worker is connected / Whether Employer, Worker, or Working on Own Account / Whether Working at Home.
6. BIRTHPLACE of every person. (1) If born in the United Kingdom, write the name of the County, and Town or Parish. (2) If born in any other part of the British Empire, write the name of the Dependency,

Colony, etc., and of the Province or State. (3) If born in a Foreign Country, write the name of the Country. (4) If born at sea, write 'At Sea'. Note – In the case of persons born elsewhere than in England or Wales, state whether 'Resident' or 'Visitor' in this Country.

7. NATIONALITY of every Person born in a Foreign Country. State whether: (1) 'British subject by parentage'. (2) 'naturalised British subject', giving year of naturalisation. Or (3) if of foreign nationality, state whether 'French', 'German', 'Russian', etc.

8. INFIRMITY. If any person included in this Schedule is: (1) 'Totally Deaf', or 'Deaf and Dumb', (2) 'Totally Blind', (3) 'Lunatic', (4) 'Imbecile', or 'Feeble-minded', state the infirmity opposite that person's name, and the age at which he or she became afflicted.

Next to the signature box at the bottom of the schedule is the box for numbers of rooms: 'Write below the number of Rooms in the Dwelling (house, Tenement or Apartment). Count the kitchen as a room but do not count scullery, landing, lobby, closet, bathroom; nor warehouse, office, shop.' The Scottish Census for 1911 was presented differently, covering two pages, but with simpler questions.

The columns regarding nationality were markedly less detailed:

Scottish Census 1911 (Glasgow ref. 644/12 005/00 021). (Reproduced with the kind permission of the Registrar General for Scotland)

1. ROAD, STREET, &c,. and No. or NAME of HOUSE
2. HOUSES./Inhabited/Uninhabited (U.) or Building (B.)
3. Rooms with one or more Windows
4. NAME and SURNAME of each Person
5. Number of Persons in House
6. RELATION to Head of Family
7. AGE (last Birthday) and Sex./Males./Females
8. Gaelic or G. & E.
9. Particulars as to Marriage/Single, Married, Widower, or Widow./ Married Women. Duration of Marriage./Children born Alive./ Children still Living
10. PROFESSION OR OCCUPATION/Personal Occupation/Industry or Service with which Worker is connected/Employer, Worker, or on Own Account/If Working at Home
11. BIRTHPLACE
12. Nationality if born in a Foreign Country
13. Whether 1. Totally Deaf or Deaf and Dumb. 2. Totally Blind. 3. Lunatic. 4. Imbecile or feeble-minded.

The Census of Ireland, 1911, Form A: 'Return of the Members of this FAMILY and their VISITORS, BOARDERS, SERVANTS, &c., who slept or abode in this House on the night of SUNDAY, the 2nd of APRIL, 1911' included similarly detailed instructions as the form of 1901. For this year, they were:

- Number [of Schedule]
- NAME and SURNAME – Christian Name/Surname
  No persons ABSENT on the night of Sunday, April 2nd, to be entered here: EXCEPT those (not enumerated elsewhere) who may be out at WORK or TRAVELLING, &c., during that Night, and who RETURN HOME ON MONDAY, APRIL 3rd/Subject to the above instruction, the Name of the Head of the Family should be written first: then the names of his Wife, Children, and other Relatives: then those of Visitors, Boarders, Servants, &c.
- RELATION to Head of Family
  State whether 'Head of Family' or 'Wife', 'Son', 'Daughter', or other Relative: 'Visitor', 'Boarder', 'Servant', &c.
- RELIGIOUS PROFESSION
  State here the particular Religion, or Religious Denomination, to which each person belongs (Members of Protestant Denominations are requested not to describe themselves by the vague term 'Protestant',

but to enter the name of the Particular Church, Denomination, or Body, to which they belong.)

- EDUCATION
State here whether he or she can 'Read and Write', can 'Read' only, or 'Cannot Read'.

- AGE (last Birthday) and SEX
Insert Age opposite each name: the Ages of Males in column 6, and the Ages of Females in column 7/For Infants under one year state the age in months, as 'under 1 month', '1 month', '2 months', &c.

- RANK, PROFESSION, OR OCCUPATION
State the Particular Rank, Profession, Trade, or other Employment of each person. Children or young persons attending a School, or receiving regular instruction at home, should be returned as *Scholars*. (No entry should be made in the case of wives, daughters, or other female relatives solely engaged in domestic duties at home.) Before filling this column you are requested to read the Instructions on the other side.

- PARTICULARS AS TO MARRIAGE
Whether 'Married', 'Widower', 'Widow', or 'Not Married'/State for each Married Woman entered on this Schedule the number of: Completed years the present Marriage has lasted. If less than one year, write 'under one'/Children born alive to present Marriage. If no children born alive, write 'None' in column 11/Total Children born alive/Children still living

- WHERE BORN
If in Ireland, state in which County or City: if elsewhere, state the name of the Country.

- IRISH LANGUAGE
Write the word 'IRISH' in this column opposite the name of each person who speaks IRISH *only*, and the words 'IRISH & ENGLISH' opposite the names of those who can speak both languages. In other cases no entry should be made in this column.

- If Deaf and Dumb; Dumb only; Blind; Imbecile or Idiot; or Lunatic
Write the respective infirmities opposite the name of the afflicted person.

Finding Aids

The English and Welsh 1911 census was released officially on 1 January 2009. This date was earlier than expected, as many had believed the census data would have to remain closed for 100 years. In fact, this requirement only came into force with the 1920 Census Act. Happily for family historians the 1911 census was not covered by the 1920 Census Act, and we were able to explore most of the information from 2009. Only personally sensitive details, such as those of infirmities or of children whose mothers were in prison, remained confidential until 2011.

As this was during the family history internet age, almost all finding aids have been published online. The Society of Genealogists published a guide to this census in 2009, written by John Hanson, entitled *How to Get the Best from the 1911 Census*.

Online Resources

This is the first census online to be reproduced in colour. The variety of colour helps to identify the different marks on the scanned schedules and provides greater legibility.

The first website to host the 1911 census images was 1911census.co.uk. This was the official 1911 census website, in association with The National Archives. This is now a partner site of Findmypast. The census can be searched for free on the 1911 website, and transcriptions viewed. Credits or a subscription are required to view the scanned image. Searches can be made via a person or place. The advanced person search hosts fields for first names, last names, year of birth, year of marriage, relationship to head, occupation, civil parish, keywords, place of birth, location (county, district or residential place), first and last names of other members of the household, or the census reference (RG 14).

The advanced location search includes fields for street, county, district, registration sub-district, residential place and census reference.

The only census website to have records, including indexes or transcriptions, of the 1911 Scottish census is ScotlandsPeople.

As with 1901, the Irish Census Website at **www.census.nationalarchives. ie** provides free access to indexes, transcriptions and scanned images of schedules for the 1911 Census of Ireland.

TheGenealogist again includes the Irish census transcriptions in the general search.

Ancestry's 1911 census collection includes the summary books. These can be used to identify the location of a house, which is useful in cases of number changes or later bomb damage. The house should first be located in the census schedules using the general or keyword search. Use the route described in the first few pages of the summary books to plot the route on a contemporary map. By pinpointing your ancestor's residence, you can also discover more about its position in the locality. As these books only give a summary of the household schedule details, the only name included is that of the head of the household. This provides a helpful overview of the householder neighbours of family members.

Unfortunately, there are limits to the indexing. This author eventually found Alfred Langford by searching with the name of the street, but a different house number. Helpfully, the book does reveal that his neighbour at 62 Regent Street was also named Mr Langford. Closer examination revealed this to be Alfred's older brother, John. The summary book also shows that the Langfords lived in a busy street, complete with the New Inn public house and a grocer's shop in their immediate vicinity. The neighbouring Sedgley Road had two public houses and a number of shops.

1911 Census entry showing Agnes Elizabeth Langford crossed out. She was living in Canada on census night (Ref. RG 13/2747/9 p.10). © Crown Copyright Images reproduced by courtesy of The National Archives, London, England www.NationalArchives.gov.uk & www.TheGenealogist.co.uk)

The infirmity columns were redacted for the release online in 2009. In January 2012, Findmypast and 1911census.co.uk published the 'infirmity' columns of the census schedules, revealing specific details of individuals' health. As with other columns in this census, householders often supplied more details than were required. The enumerator of Harting in Hampshire put two red lines through the infirmity entry of 26-year-old Thomas Wallace Young: the naval officer's entry, in pencil or light ink, reads 'Bald & Toothless'.[5]

Others revealed illnesses or infirmities in the occupation column. The 39-year-old Clara Cuckow in Warnham, Sussex, for example, gave her profession as 'Invalid (Rhumatoid [*sic*] Arthritis)'.[6] For 2009–2012, this column was censored for data protection reasons. These census providers also then revealed the details of children under 3 born to women in prison. At the time of writing, not all census providers had released this information.

The National Archives' reference code for the 1911 census is RG 14.

Free Resources

The indexes on 1911census.co.uk and Findmypast are free. FamilySearch provides free indexes and transcriptions but links to Findmypast to view the images.

NRS provides thirty-one street indexes to towns and cities across Scotland at **https://www.nrscotland.gov.uk/research/guides/census-records/1911-census#occupations**.

The only census website to offer completely full access to its records is **www.census.nationalarchives.ie**.

The FreeCen website does not cover the 1911 census.

Problems

Although the accuracy of the 1911 census transcriptions is regarded as very good, there are some errors. There are no missing household schedules, but there are missing enumerator summary books.

The affected parishes are as follows:

- Beaconsfield in Buckinghamshire
- Parson Drove, Tydd St Giles and West Walton (part) in Cambridgeshire
- Lymm in Cheshire
- Okehampton in Devonshire
- Calthoroe, Colesbaych, Shawell, Swinford, Westrill and Starmore in Leicestershire
- Sutton St Edmund and Tydd St Mary in Lincolnshire
- Brislington (part), Whitchurch and Bishopsworth in Somerset
- Brethey, Bolehall and Glascote in Staffordshire
- Atherstone, Witherly and Fenny Drayton in Warwickshire.

Suffragism was reaching its height in 1911. Answering the Women's Freedom League's call of 'No Votes for Women – No Census', hundreds of women boycotted the census in protest at their lack of suffrage. Some wrote 'No Vote, No Census' on their schedules. Others are either not enumerated at all or reveal limited detail (some refused to give their names). Eighty-two of these women can be identified by using the keyword 'vote' on TheGenealogist's master search of this census.

Emily Wilding Davison would become notorious in the history of women's suffrage when, on 4 June 1913, she was struck by the king's horse while trying to throw a suffragette banner over him during the Epsom Derby and died from her injuries four days later. In 1911, she was one of thousands of British women involved in the suffragette movement. Instead of boycotting the census by refusing to complete her details on the household schedule, Davison snuck into the House of Commons on the night of the census to mark her protest. She tried to use the House of Commons as the location where she was enumerated as 'Emily Wilding Davidson' with an extra 'd'. Her address on the census is 'Crypt of Westminster Hall'. Davison gave her details as 35, single and a schoolteacher, born in Long Worsley, Northumberland (ref. RG14/5/3/24/74, p.489). In 1991, Tony Benn MP placed a plaque in the Chapel of St Mary Undercroft in honour of Davison and her overnight visit.

1911 Census entry for Emily Wilding Davison in the Houses of Parliament. (© Crown Copyright Images reproduced by courtesy of The National Archives, London, England. www.NationalArchives.gov.uk & www.TheGenealogist.co.uk)

In a more typical protest, Women's Social and Political Union (WSPU) organizer Dorothy Bowker of 7 York Street, Marylebone, London defaced her paper. She explained her boycott by writing:

'No Vote – No Census. I am Dumb politically. Blind to the Census. Deaf to Enumerators. Being classed with criminals lunatics & paupers I prefer to give no further particulars.'

1911 Dorothy Bowker. (© Crown Copyright Images reproduced by courtesy of The National Archives, London, England. www.NationalArchives.gov.uk & www.TheGenealogist.co.uk)

More can be found on suffragette ancestors in the collections at the Women's Library and on Elizabeth Crawford's Woman and Her Sphere website: **https://womanandhersphere.com/2014/05/14/suffrage-stories-1911-census-view-house-of-commons-talk-vanishing-for-the-vote-the-suffragette-boycott/**.[7]

Women would not gain the vote for another seven years. Yet this was a success for the suffragettes in that none were prosecuted. The boycott was a peaceful protest which drew the attention of government and the public to the cause of women's suffrage. Nevertheless, the lack of sympathy with which the cause was viewed by some contemporaries is evident in this mocking poem published in the *Penny Illustrated Paper* (a cheap weekly news sheet) two months before the census was taken:[8]

THE MOTIVE? Oh, Suffragette,
Wilt ever let
Thine angry passions rise? Thy little hands,

One understands,

Have clawed policemen's eyes; And now to fill our sorrow's cup,
   Thou wilt not fill thy paper up! With eyes aflame

Thou play'st a game, That is not nice to see: With fearsome zest
   Thou dost thy best

To picket each M.P.

And now thy wild ambitions burn To burke the census-man's
   return. On sorry nags

Thou bearest flags Along our busy roads, Nor dost relax

Absurd attacks

On Ministers' abodes

And boycotting the census seems To be the latest of thy schemes.
   Oh, Suffragette!

Thou shouldst not let Thyself thus misbehave, And in my heart

Of hearts I start

To have suspicions grave,

That thou upon the census page

Art disinclined to state thine age.

1911 Census Cover of Coseley, Staffordshire.

How to Use the Census Effectively

This census became known as the fertility census as a result of its length of marriage and number of children columns. Although they were used at the time to establish the fertility of the population, the details given are of immense value to family historians.

Genealogists also benefit from the mistakes made by householders who were unsure about what to include. The example on page 154 shows the Langford family of 62 Regent Street, Woodsetton, near Dudley in the West Midlands. The schedule was completed by the father of the family, 52-year- old ironworker Alfred Langford. He and his wife, Sarah Matilda, had produced nine children in their years of marriage. Alfred either did not know how many years they had been married, or somehow missed this column. As was required, Alfred wrote the number of those children who had died – two – but did not give their names. Seemingly confused about the seven children who were still living, Alfred named all of them on the form. What is particularly helpful about this is that in his mistake he reveals what has happened to his three eldest daughters.

'What happened to the daughters?' is a common question raised by family historians. It can be very difficult to prove that a woman is unmarried or married, or to identify whether she died or went abroad. In this example, we learn that Harriet Louisa and Emmie Gertrude are married, although their new surnames are not given, and we discover that Agnes Elizabeth Langford is abroad. Even more helpfully, we learn that while living 'abroad', Agnes is working as a 'General Servant Domestic'. Using this information, the author was able to search further for Agnes, trying to work out where she was likely to have emigrated. The author searched the ships' passages out on Findmypast and discovered that a few months earlier, on 28 July 1910, Agnes had travelled to Montreal in Canada under the auspices of the Salvation Army. Conveniently, a census was taken in Canada in June 1911, and it was possible to find Agnes working as a domestic servant, just as her father had said, in the Royal Victoria Hospital, Montreal. Without Alfred's error, this was likely to have proved a much more unfocused and time-consuming search.

The question over children also confused the Filbert family of Clapton Park in London. Their daughter, 22-year-old Margaret, was enumerated as a 21-year-old servant living in a nearby Islington laundry (ref. RG14/976, p.782). Despite this, Margaret's father, 45-year-old gardening labourer William Filbert, recorded her as being present in the family home. He described her as 'General Servant – Laundry', confirming the evidence of her first census entry. He also wrote the names of his four children who had died. These were later crossed out, though they are still legible, providing useful genealogical detail (ref. RG14/1099, p.518).

One detail to look out for is the number written in red next to the box marked '(To be filled up by the Enumerator)' on the bottom left of the schedule. This is the enumerator's confirmation of the total number of children under 10 in the household. If this number is different from that given by the householder, this may suggest one of the young children has died.

Occasionally, a green figure appears next to the red figure. This indicates the number of servants in the household.

Other green numbers and dashes are found in the 'Profession or Occupation' column. These numbers are (from left to right) the occupational codes, the industry codes and the status codes. They can be matched against the official lists. Copies of these lists can be found on the Findmypast website at **https://www.findmypast.co.uk/content/ expert-1911-occupation-codes** and a scan of the original code sheet can be seen on HISTPOP in *Census of England, Wales and Islands in the British Seas, 1911*, page 1: 'Forms used by clerks for abstracting and tabling of census data'. The census occupation codes for Scotland can be found on the HISTPOP website.

The enumerators were required to note the numbers of scholars and students engaged in occupations who attended school or other instructional classes (full-time, half-time or part-time). Aside from occupational data, the enumerators recorded the number of tenements with more than two occupants per room.

The schedule used numbers written in green in the birthplace column. These are the codes for birthplaces and can be found in the census report form on page 10. Visitors were given a different code from residents. As can be seen in the example of the Langford family's schedule, not all enumerators observed this instruction.

Taking it Further

The 1911 census may be one of the last surviving records of men and women who served in the First World War of 1914–18. Almost all of the 9 million men and women who are believed to have served in British forces during the war will be found in the census. Unfortunately, only around 40 per cent of the records survive from this war, and of those that exist many are faded or damaged by fire from an air raid in 1940. Nevertheless, where records do survive, they can be compared with the details revealed in the 1911 census in order to corroborate or disprove identity. British army service, pension and medal records from the war can be found on Ancestry. The National Archives holds records for those who served in other areas. A selection of service records for the Royal Navy and Royal Air Force can be searched online via Discovery.

Army nurses' records can be downloaded via **https://www.national archives.gov.uk/help-with-your-research/research-guides/british-army-nurses-service-records-1914-1918/** and Women's Army Auxiliary Corps records from **www.nationalarchives.gov.uk/records/womens-army-auxiliary-corps.htm**. Transcriptions of other military nurses' records can be viewed at Findmypast. Those for the Indian army are held at the British Library. Other useful records and items can be found at the Imperial War Museum. The Long, Long Trail website, **www.1914-1918.net**, contains detailed information on regiments, battles, formations and maps.

The surviving census summary books can be used to discover more about an ancestor's neighbourhood and home. The 'number of rooms' box on the schedule gives some insight into the size of the property, and investigations on contemporary maps can provide further details.

Even more details of a property around 1911 may be found in surviving records of the Valuation Office survey of 1910–15. Sometimes referred to as a census or 'Lloyd George's Domesday', the survey was taken under the 1909/10 Finance Act. An assessment of all properties in Britain, the survey was used to support the Act's aim of levying a tax on part of the profit of a sale of property. For the survey, England and Wales were divided into 118 valuation districts and then parishes.

The surviving records include field books and plans (maps) drawn up after valuation; these are held at TNA. The survey maps can be found via this online tool from TNA's website: **http://labs.nationalarchives. gov.uk/wordpress/index.php/2010/04/valuation-office-map-finder**. The relevant field book can be found via the respective plan. The books reveal the names of the owner and occupier, the type of holding, terms of any tenancy, area covered by property, and the market value. The valuation or 'Domesday' books and some working plans survive in local record offices. Those for the cities of London and Westminster are held at TNA. Scottish valuation records are held at the National Archives of Scotland (NAS) and those for Ireland at the NAI.

Unique Features of the Non-English Censuses

For this year, the Irish census includes numbers of children who have died. Users of the Irish census website can search on this for mortality figures across a county, for example. Again, the Irish census is unique in asking for details of religion, and being specific in that 'Members of the Protestant Denominations are requested not to describe themselves by the general term "Protestant" but to enter the name of the Particular Church, Denomination, or Body to which they belong.' The initial summaries of the Irish census estimated that 3,238,656, or 73.9 per cent of the population were Roman Catholic, 575,489 were Protestant Episcopalians, 439,876 Presbyterian and 61,806 Methodist.[9]

In Scotland, the Registrar General took information for the census report from the CEBs rather than the household schedules. The Scottish report was finished by the end of 1913.

An online exhibition of life in 1911 Belfast can be viewed at **www.belfastfamilyhistory.com/exhibition.php**.

Summary

In 1911 the most radical changes took place to the enumeration process, and this can be one of the most revealing censuses. There were new Registrars General in England and Wales, Scotland and Ireland. In England and Wales, Mallet and Stevenson took a confident approach to the census, introducing new questions that reflected their and other social scientists' interest in eugenics. These also built on the nation's fears regarding immigration and a middle-class concern over high numbers of working-class births. In other ways, Mallet and Stevenson misjudged the national mood, being unprepared for the boycott by suffragettes and perhaps unprepared for the political agitation that would develop later in the year.

In this coronation year, great change was just beginning. After the Great War of 1914–18, British society would be radically altered. The changes wrought by war would affect future census administration and interrupt the reporting of the 1911 census. Besides this, the war would see hundreds of thousands of men on this census sent to their deaths.

Chapter 11

LATER CENSUSES

History of the Census up to 1945

During the war, in August 1915, a national register was created of men and women aged between 16 and 65. All persons were to sign up to the register on 15 August. The purpose of this was to establish the availability of men and women for war service or work. Its consequence was the introduction of conscription in January 1916. Unfortunately for genealogists, none of the records of this registration survive.

Throughout the war, Bernard Mallet remained as Registrar General, eventually retiring in 1920. His successor, Sylvanus Percival Vivian, would become the longest-serving Registrar General after George Graham, remaining in post until 1945.

The Census Act of 1920 was a radical departure from previous Acts in that it established not just the census of 1921, but the census as a regular decennial event. No longer would each census require a separate Act of Parliament. Censuses would be established by an Order in Council, giving the date and details requested. Besides this, the Act made the census office a permanent fixture. The role of the superintendent registrars was reduced to that of mere consultation, but they were granted the title of census advisory officer. Interestingly, the Act made provision for a quinquennial census. Since the Victorian age, there had been calls for censuses to be taken every five years from a number of individual and institutions, not least London County Council, who wanted an accurate estimation of the population, 'especially for the purposes of the London (Equalization of Rates) Act, 1894'.[1] It was argued that London's population changed considerably within just five years. Despite some sympathy shown to the idea of quinquennial census, particularly by Neville Chamberlain in the late 1920s, no complete five-year census of Britain was taken in the twentieth century.

Unfortunately, the plans went awry almost immediately. Census night had been set for 24 April 1921, but industrial unrest led to its postponement in England, Wales and Scotland until 19 June. New questions were introduced. One of the most useful to family historians was that of divorce.

The infirmity column no longer asked for blind, or deaf and dumb. Perhaps sadly for family historians, the fertility question was not included. The *Census for England and Wales 1921, Preliminary Report* revealed a total population of 37,885,242, a small increase from 1911. The report acknowledged, though, that comparisons between the 1911 and 1921 censuses were confused by the population movement of the Great War and the influenza pandemic that followed:

> The number of arrivals and departures to and from this country of members of the British Forces, of the Forces of the Dominions, Colonies and Allied Powers, of enemy prisoners and war refugees amounted to many millions; and though, after allowing for the deaths which occurred abroad and the known excess of non-civilians outside England and Wales in 1921 as compared with 1911, the exits and entries may be expected to have tended to neutralise one another (p.x).

Overall, the results of this census showed the impact of the war on birth rates. Also, there was now a greater imbalance of males to females, with more than 700,000 males having died in the war. In Scotland, the 1921 population was 4,882,288; the smallest growth in fifty years. As in England and Wales, females far exceeded males, though it was in England that the difference was greatest, with 1,101 females to 1,000 males.

The Times suggested a solution for this: 'active' women should migrate to the Dominions. An article published on Tuesday, 30 August 1921 (p.9) reported:

> Our Correspondent showed that, upon a rough computation, there is an excess of only 50,000 marriageable men in the Commonwealth of Australia, 12,000 in New Zealand, 30,000 in South Africa, and 20,000 in Canada…. [But] So long as the proportion of men to women in the Dominions is higher than in this country the opportunities of marriage open to women there must be greater than here….

The census report for that year introduced tables comparing the populations of the key parts of the British Empire: Australia, New Zealand, India, South Africa and Canada. The Canadian Census for 1921 was released to the Library and Archives Canada (LAC) on 1 June 2013 from Statistics Canada. The census can be searched online at the Library and Archives' website: **https://www.bac-lac.gc.ca/eng/census/1921/Pages/search.aspx**. It is expected to be online a few months later. Previous censuses can be searched at **www.collectionscanada.gc.ca** and **www.ancestry.ca**. Women also sought husbands in the USA. Luckily for family historians, some or all of the US censuses up to 1940 are available to search online at a number of websites, including Ancestry.com, FamilySearch and 1940census.archives.gov, with instructions available at **www.census.gov**.

The 1921 census of England, Wales and the 'Islands in the British Seas' will be released by The National Archives in January 2022. The Scottish census should be online in summer 2021. Findmypast won the contract to publish the census in January 2022. Questions were different from earlier censuses, with children being asked whether their mother or their father or both were dead in the wake of the First World War. However, in contrast with the Fertility Census of 1911, the 1921 census asked only how many children or stepchildren the family had, and how many were still alive. This census was the first to ask whether a marriage had been dissolved by divorce. Merchant ships in English and Welsh waters, all Royal Navy ships, and army and RAF units stantioned overseas are all recorded. Interestingly, for occupational and social historians this census also asks about workplaces, which can help to identify the names of those with whom respondents worked. Like the census of 1841, this census took place in June. Originally, the census was planned for late April, but a coal miners' strike led to its postponement.[2]

A full entry on a standard household schedule will contain:

- full address of the property
- names of persons in each household
- relationship to head of household
- age (this was now required as years and completed months, rather than just years as in previous censuses)
- sex
- "marriage or orphanhood"
  - For those aged 15 and over this field recorded if you were single, married, or widowed, and for the first time D was to be recorded for those whose marriage had been dissolved by divorce
  - For those under 15 this recorded if both parents were alive, father dead, mother dead or both dead.
  - This field will again show the impact of the First World War with a greater proportion of widows recorded than in 1911, and 730,000 children recorded with "Father dead" versus 260,000 with "Mother dead".

- place of birth and, nationality for those born outside the UK
- occupation and employment
  - if in whole or part-time education
- principally for recording those at school or university, but could also include adults taking evening classes
  - Employment
- For those employed, name and type of employer, otherwise recording "employer", or "own account". Those out of work are instructed to give their last employee and add "out of work"
  - Place of Work – employer's address (except for those in private employment such as domestic service
- Number of children or stepchildren under the age of 16
  - To be filled in by married men, widowers and widows, a total number followed by a cross in a box for each age that was applicable to a child or stepchild.

Unique features of the non-English 1921 censuses are that in Wales and the Isle of Man a column was added for an additional language (Welsh/Manx, English, or Both). The armed forces schedule also asks if the person can speak Welsh or Gaelic (in addition to English). This could be useful for discovering more about the language skills of ancestors who grew up in England in Welsh or Manx migrant families.

Civil war in Ireland prevented the census from taking place there in 1921. However, those with ancestors in 1920s Ireland may find them in the Army Census of the National Army (of the Irish Free State), which took place on the night of 12 November 1922 during the Civil War/War of Independence. The original census records comprise ten bound volumes of census returns and are held at the Military Archives in Dublin. The census has been digitized and can be searched by forename and/or surname at the Defences Ireland website: **http://www.militaryarchives. ie/collections/online-collections/irish-army-census-collection-12- november-1922-13-november-1922.**

The transcription gives the location of the person on 12 November 1922, as well as the name, age, page and a download link to a PDF of the relevant census file. The scanned image provides plenty of useful genealogical details in the columns: regimental no., rank, corps, name, age, home address, no. on pay book, date of attestation, place of attestation, married or single, religion, next of kin, name and address of next of kin and remarks.

It was only on 18 April 1926 that a census was able to take place in Ireland and Northern Ireland. The returns of the Irish Free State are held by the NAI, while those of Northern Ireland are believed to have been destroyed in the Second World War. It is believed that the 1926 Irish census will be released online in 2027. The reports for the census of Northern Ireland can be read at HISTPOP.

In England and Wales, Vivian was keen to modernize the census, and used the event of the 26 April 1931 enumeration to tell the nation about the process, through a series of BBC wireless broadcasts. A new question was introduced, asking for the usual residence. This, and its supplementary question of employer's address, would have been very useful to family historians. In this year, interpreters were sent to areas of high immigrant populations, such as the Chinese and to the Yiddish-speaking Jewish families of London's East End. To mark the occasion of a new census, the Public Record Office created an exhibition, similar to recent displays at the British Library and other archives, on the history of the census, showing old census returns. The results of that year's census revealed a noticeable fall in the birth rate. Many family historians will notice a change in the size of their families in the twentieth century. Parents who had at least six siblings each would deliberately restrict their own family size to two or three children. Women continued to outnumber men: in England and Wales the number of females was 1,670,243 higher than that of males. Sadly for family historians, the English and Welsh 1931 census returns were destroyed in 1942. Happily, the Scottish census returns survive as they were stored separately in Edinburgh.

A census took place in the Republic of Ireland in 1936 and in Northern Ireland on 28 February 1937. The surviving returns are held at NAI and PRONI respectively, but remain closed to the public.

In 1941, the census was not taken. Britain was in the midst of war, with many areas suffering regular aerial bombing. Instead of supervising a decennial census in this decade, Registrar General Vivian was given responsibility for the national registration scheme of identity cards. The records Vivian created were subsequently destroyed, but individual identity cards do survive in local archives, museums such as the Imperial War Museum and in private collections.

With no surviving census from the 1930s or 1940s, family historians have turned to the 1939 register. This national register of residents of the United Kingdom, Northern Ireland and the Isle of Man was created by the National Registration Act of 1939, which was repealed on 22 May 1952. The Second World War began on 1 September 1939. On 29 September 1939, a national survey was taken of the civilian population. Although it was not officialy a census, some citizens did regard it as such. On 18 September 1939, *The Scotsman* (page 6) reported, 'Every person in

Screengrab of the 1911census.org.uk website showing a blank schedule of the 1939 National Registration.

Great Britain and Northern Ireland will be entered in Britain's war-time census on National Registration Day, which has been fixed for Friday, September 29.' Members of the armed services were not included in the register as it was not meant to record members of the armed forces. However, the records do include members of the armed services on leave and civilians on military bases.

Data was collected into national registration transcription books by around 65,000 enumerators during the evening of national registration day, Friday, 29 September 1939. The process mirrored that of the census, with forms being handed out to householders, then being collected and checked by the enumerators on the following Sunday and Monday. During the collection process, the enumerators issued completed identity cards for each resident. Thus, anyone who did not register would not receive an identity card. Officially, this survey was carried out to understand the size of the population, particularly of potential servicemen and women, confirm identification (national security in a time of war), and to prepare for the likely introduction of food rationing. The returns were sent to local food officers for them to issue ration books. Another purpose was to ensure members of families did not lose contact. As history would prove, this last aim was not always successful.[3]

On 2 November 2015, Findmypast in partnership with The National Archives[4] made digitally scanned versions of the enumerators' transcript books for the 1939 Register for England and Wales available to search online. In theory, individuals' records remain closed for 100 years from their date of birth or until proof of death is produced. However, there are

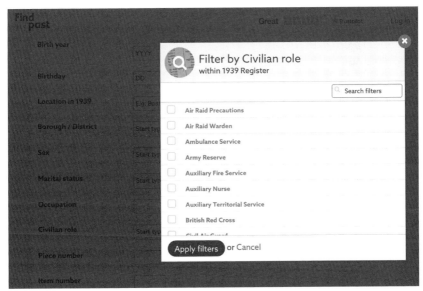

Page on the Findmypast website from 1939 Register showing entries for Stepney in London.

FindmyPast has now transcribed and created classifications for wartime civilian roles. These include Air Raid Precautions, Civil Nursing Reserve, Decontamination Squad, Fire Brigade, and National Pigeon Service. This search option enables researchers to browse or filter by keyword from the 'See Instructions' column on the second page of each register image.

examples where this is not the case. These records are redacted on the digital images. Closed records should thus be blanked out in the search results. The online sites annually add records with birth dates older than 100 years, and where a record of death (for those who have died since 1939, but whose birth anniversary has not yet been reached) has been reported to The National Archives.

The National Archives' reference code for this register is RG 101.

Problems

There are often problems with the dates of birth given on this register. It is possible that older people or children not living with close relatives did not know their full birth date. There are also many examples of individuals giving the wrong year. In the case of those in their late thirties, this may have been in an attempt to reduce their chances of eligibility for military conscription. Also, some women who are known to have been in paid work at the time have their occupations recorded with the generic term 'Unpaid Domestic Duties'. Thus, the accuracy of entries should be checked against other sources.

Some entries in the register are incomplete or have faded to the point of illegibility.

The following details are provided for a person living in England and Wales at the time the survey was taken:

- National registration number
- Address
- Surname
- First forename
- Other forename(s)/initial(s)
- Date of birth
- Sex
- Marital status (including divorced)
- Occupation.

As this was a record of the civilian population, the records do not feature the following:

- British army barracks
- Royal Navy stations
- Royal Air Force stations
- Members of the armed forces billeted in homes, including their own homes.

An unintentionally useful feature of the Register is that, as it was used from 1948 as the basis of the National Health Service Register, some extra information may be recorded against an individual. This includes names being crossed out with another name written in an annotation above or at the side, particularly in the cases of married women. It is therefore worth searching the register with both the married name and the maiden name of a woman who married after September 1939.

Other notes featured on the right-hand side of the register image record details such as whether an individual had volunteered as an air-raid warden.

For Scotland, applications should be made to the GROS. Application forms are available via the webpage: **https://www.nrscotland.gov.uk/statistics-and-data/nhs-central-register/about-the-register/1939-national-identity-register-and-how-to-order-an-official-extract**.

Records from the Isle of Man are not known to survive.

For Northern Ireland, information can be received free of charge from PRONI via an application made under the Freedom of Information (FOI) Act **https://www.nidirect.gov.uk/forms/proni-enquiry**.

What is Available Now?

England	Wales	Isle of Man	Channel Islands	Scotland	Ireland	Northern Ireland
Census reports 1921 and 1931				Census reports 1921 and 1931	Census reports 1926 and 1936	Census reports 1926 and 1937
1939 Register online	–		–	1939 Register service	–	1939 Register service

The 1939 Register can now be searched online at Findmypast, Ancestry and MyHeritage. The index can be searched for free on FamilySearch, with users being directed to images on Findmypast.

What will be Available in the Future?

England	Wales	Isle of Man	Channel Islands	Scotland	Ireland	Northern Ireland
1921 Census schedules	1921 Census schedules	1921 Census schedules	1921 Census schedules	1921 and 1931 schedules	1926 and 1936 schedules	1937 Census schedules

Chapter 12

THE CENSUS TODAY

Census Recording Between 1945 and 2020

The Census Act of 1920 had legislated for regular decennial censuses in England and Wales and, finally, from 1951 this was what occurred. Censuses took place in Scotland, Ireland and Northern Ireland on the same day, Sunday, 8 April. That year's census reintroduced a fertility question, enquiring as to the length of present marriage, number of children born alive during the marriage, and whether a child had been born to the marriage in the past twelve months.

In the Republic of Ireland, meanwhile, a quinquennial census had taken place in 1946. This was followed by the census of 1951 and then another in 1956.

In 1961, computers were first used in census-taking. Although the mechanical tabulation introduced in 1911 had become more sophisticated over time, the process was still controlled by humans. From 1961, the processing of census data became automatic. An IBM 705, originally bought to maintain soldiers' pay records for the Royal Army Pay Corps, was used to compute the data.[1] The censuses of England, Wales, Scotland, Ireland and Northern Ireland now asked more questions on fertility, with numbers of live children born to widows and divorced women. In a time of increasing numbers of divorces, the census also asked women if they had been married more than once.[2]

In 1966, besides the census of Ireland, some households in England, Wales, Scotland and Northern Ireland took part in a quinquennial census. This was a sample census, using only 10 per cent of addresses from the 1961 census, along with 10 per cent of new dwellings from the local authorities' ratifying lists. For this year, the fertility question was removed.

The 1971 census of England, Wales, Scotland, Ireland and Northern Ireland asked for all dates of birth of all children born live in a marriage,

Appendix I 1971 Census form (private households)   *1971 Census Form.*

and for the date of first marriage (and of termination, if ended). In a rare interruption of the regular census-taking, the quinquennial census of Ireland of 1976 was cancelled for economic reasons, and an extra census was held there in 1979.

In a reversal of decades of census practice, the 1981 census of England, Wales, Scotland, Ireland and Northern Ireland contained fewer questions than those in 1971. Some were removed by the direct intervention of the then prime minister, Margaret Thatcher.[3] The quinquennial census of Ireland and Northern Ireland was restored in 1986. Five years later, the 1991 census of England, Wales, Scotland, Ireland and Northern Ireland included three extra questions on ethnic group, limiting long-term illness and the term-time address of students. Also, a question on central heating was added to the household amenities section. In 1996, a quinquennial census was again undertaken in Ireland and Northern Ireland.

The Casweb online database **http://casweb.mimas.ac.uk** has digitized reports for English, Scottish and Welsh censuses between 1971 and 2001.

Those for Northern Ireland can be read at the NISRA website **https:// www.nisra.gov.uk/statistics/census**.

Reports for the census of the Republic of Ireland for 1926–91 are online at **https://www.cso.ie/en/census/**

Post-War Censuses and Family History

During the later twentieth century, the storage of the census books was radically improved, paving the way for the opening up of census material to the public, and their use by family historians. In 1962, the CEBs for the 1861 census were sent to the Public Record Office. The books of the 1851 census had been deposited originally with the Public Record Office in 1854, but the Registrar General asked for them to be returned. By 1862, the office had custody of the 1801–31 returns, but those for 1841 and 1861 were mislaid. In 1904, the 1841 and 1861 censuses were found in the Houses of Parliament. Five years later the Scottish census returns for 1841 and 1851 were sent to Edinburgh. In 1912, the 1851 CEBs were sent finally to be stored with the other sets of books at the Public Record Office.[4]

Censuses of 2001 and 2011

In 2001, keen to have some understanding of the enumeration process of the past, I applied to work on the census. For the first time, the process was run by the Office for National Statistics (ONS), which had been formed five years earlier in a merger of the Central Statistical Office (CSO), the Office of Population Censuses and Surveys (OPCS) and the statistics division of the Department of Employment. I would be one of around 63,000 enumerators who worked on the census that year.

I applied late in the process and was sent to an expensive area of London, which needed new recruits. My fellow enumerators were a mixed bunch; certainly not the altruistic professionals desired by George Graham. Most were motivated by money, or at least the opportunity for temporary part-time work, but some wanted to do something different and interesting. Our first meeting involved gathering in a large hall among an untidy assortment of papers, boxes and bright yellow plastic bags. We were introduced to our supervisors and placed into teams. The slogan for this census was 'Count me in', and there was a general air of cheeriness. Each team was to enumerate a specific section of the district, and each enumerator given flat and house numbers within named streets. For our first task, we went out together as a team, each of us carrying a heavy bag of householder schedules and a clipboard. We distributed the census packs, handing them to each householder (or whoever was available) and explaining how to complete the form. For each household, we had to note the name of the householder on our records. From then on we had to return, on our own, until each schedule was delivered; ideally before the census night of 29 April. Where there was no answer after two visits we would ask neighbours where the residents were and post the form through any available letterbox.

Most of my households were in an exclusive block of flats. Luckily for me, these flats had a very friendly full-time porter who was able to give me all the details I needed. Like the female enumerators of the 1891 census, I experienced some suspicion from residents who were reluctant to tell me anything about themselves in fear of how it would be used. However, they were a minority. The main problems I encountered were residents who lived most of their time away from the address, second home-owners, and confused au pairs. One woman refused to answer the door, but, hearing the television inside, I refused to leave. It turned out she was a horse-owner and each time I'd visited she'd been watching the racing. Others were more pleasant, inviting me in to sit comfortably while I filled out the forms and offering me drinks and biscuits. The specifics of this enumeration district strongly affected my experience of working as an enumerator. It highlighted to me that when examining my ancestors' census entries, it is essential to have prior understanding of the localities in which they lived. It also showed that some of the problems experienced by the earliest enumerators had continued into the twenty-first century.

Many of the difficulties I experienced in this Inner London borough were common in other urban areas. According to a report published in 2010,[5] the City of Westminster (not the borough where I enumerated) is one of the most difficult in which to take the census:

> Those enumerators tasked with filling in the gaps left by the postal survey, are likely to find themselves confronted by a multitude of physical and cultural barriers, from oblique buzzer-entry systems, to diffident, suspicious or unwilling respondents. And in many cases, enumerators simply could not find entrances and doorways at all (p.4).

Other problems highlighted were the 'large number of residents [who] did not speak English', the 'fast-changing nature of the population', 'bad weather and hours of time spent without success' and 'a desire for the work to come to an end quickly'. I experienced a number of these in my time as an enumerator and they would have been familiar to many of the enumerators of cities from the late nineteenth century onwards. Anyone who has studied the Victorian censuses of Soho, Marylebone, Paddington and Millbank will appreciate that contemporary enumerators probably felt something similar.

In Ireland, the spread of foot and mouth disease in Ireland led to the delay of the 2001 census until 2002. However, the census in Northern Ireland went ahead on 29 April 2001, as in the rest of the UK.

The 2001 census asked forty-one questions, seven more than in 1991. One of the most controversial was a voluntary question on religion. This was the first time a question on religion had been asked on the main census form (outside Ireland). In New Zealand, where a similar question was asked, a campaign grew, urging respondents to register their religion as Jedi, the fictitious religion of the *Star Wars* films. In Britain, many seized on this as a way of reacting against the religion question; others just thought it would be funny to describe themselves as Jedis. In fact, so many respondents (390,217) gave their faith as Jedi that it was recorded as the fourth most popular religion in England and Wales. In 2011, the Humanist Society organized another campaign asking the non-religious to write 'no religion' rather than Jedi. Consequently, numbers of recorded Jedis fell.

Scottish households were unique in Britain that year for being asked the address of the place of study and means of travel to the place of study. Only English households were asked for details of professional qualifications. This census received great criticism both in the media and among households. Having worked on it, I agree with those who claim the process was disorganized. Our team regularly complained that we were working in chaos. This census was also more expensive than any in the history of the process, costing an estimated £254 million.[6] These problems of chaos and cost are major factors in what some commentators believe will be the likely demise of the UK census. Clearly, sometime between 1881 and 2001, the UK census procedure had lost the efficiency that had led to its description as 'the perfection of modern administrative machinery'.[7]

In 2011, there was again much criticism of the census questions. There was confusion over question 17, which was left blank in England but asked about Welsh language for households in Wales. Other criticisms were that the name section did not ask for middle names, the answer options for the question on employment did not include 'retired', and there was no option for recording voluntary work.

Some genealogists have kept copies of the 2001 and 2011 censuses, either as paper copies or scanned and saved on computer hard drives, floppy discs or CDs. In 2011, there was some discussion among family historians as to how best to store their personal census records. Most agreed that making a copy of the census would benefit their descendants so that, unlike them, they would not have to wait 100 years to see the details. Some of the interesting blog posts on this topic can be read online at **http://cmgurney.blogspot.co.uk/2011/03/genealogist-view-of-2011-census.html**, **www.hibbitt.org.uk/blog/item/233/category/19** and **http:// chrispatonsblog.blogspot.com/2011/03/census-day-2011.html**.

The 2011 census took place on 27 March 2011. It was organized by the Office for National Statistics (ONS) in England and Wales, the General Register Office for Scotland, and the Northern Ireland Statistics and Research Agency. The census papers were posted to each household from the beginning of March, when everyone in England and Wales was asked to complete and return the questionnaire. For the first time the questionnaire could be completed online using a unique access code. Householders could post the completed schedules in their own time: as long as the information related to the household on census night, a late return was acceptable. The statistical results of this census are available through the dedicated webpage **https://www.ons.gov.uk/ census/2011census/2011censusdata**.

Copying census data is something family historians in New Zealand have been doing for some time. All censuses taken there, from the first in 1851 to that of 1991, were routinely destroyed. Since 2005, legislation ensures that the censuses are retained, but that they remain closed for 100 years. Even then, the census forms can only be used for statistical purposes. Unless the law is changed, no personal details from them will be disclosed to the public. The 2011 New Zealand census was due to be taken on 8 March. This was postponed by the devastating Canterbury / Christchurch earthquakes which left many homeless or in temporary accommodation. The census eventually went ahead on Tuesday, 5 March 2013, in the post and online, but only those who have taken copies will leave details for their descendants.

In Australia, too, census copying is common among family historians. Few original census records there survive. Between 1971 and 1996, census forms (in paper and electronic form) were routinely destroyed after the required statistics had been extracted. Since 2001, those householders wishing for their details to be archived by the National Archives of Australia have the option of requesting this via a tick box. All census forms left unticked are destroyed.

Future Plans

For 200 years, there have been criticisms of the census, many on grounds of intrusion. Nevertheless, in 2001 only 1,500 households failed to complete the form and of these only 37 were prosecuted. Despite this, the government views the exercise as costly and old-fashioned. In 2010, the Cabinet Office Minister Francis Maude suggested scrapping the census altogether, arguing, 'there are, I believe, ways of doing this which will provide better, quicker information, more frequently and cheaper.'

The ONS began looking at other methods that could achieve the same ends. A statement from the Office in 2011 reads: 'In the UK the National Statistician has set up "Beyond 2011" programme to establish and test models for meeting future users' needs for census-type statistics, including socio-demographic variables. This programme starts on 1st April and proposals will be made in 2014.'[8]

The General Register Office for Scotland was also looking at different census options as part of their 'Beyond 2011' enquiry. These included:

- a short form of basic demographic details plus a long form / traditional census for a small sample of the population
- a rolling census – surveying the population in stages
- administrative data plus a small percentage of full survey (either annually or decennially).

Others argued that useful statistical data can be gained from other, cheaper sources such as the forty-year-old general household survey. Like the census, this is organized by the Office for National Statistics, but surveys a smaller percentage of the population.

However, preparation has now been made for Census 2021. The Office for National Statistics (ONS) held a census rehearsal in October 2019 in order to ensure that their processes, systems and services are running smoothly. Four areas – Carlisle, Ceredigion, Hackney and Tower Hamlets – were chosen to rehearse the census as together they represented a good cross-section of contemporary society.

As with previous censuses, the one being planned for March 2021 will be different from those of earlier decades. There will be some change in the questions asked and, most significantly, this will be a 'digital-first' census. Organizers hope for as many householders as possible to fill their questionnaire online in 2021. Full details can be found on the official Census 2021 website: **https://census.gov.uk**.

In 2011, Andrew Miller, the Labour MP for Ellesmere Port and Leston, and the chair of the House of Commons Science and Technology Select

Committee, argued, 'The census has provided the UK with one of the richest collections of population data in the world. It is incredibly valuable to social researchers, charities and the public sector and a move to cancel the census on financial grounds may prove to be a costly mistake.'[9]

Miller's words echo those of John Rickman, the founder of the modern census, written long ago in 1796: 'It will be intuitively granted that an intimate knowledge of a country can be the only foundation of the legislation of that country, and also of its political relation to other nations.'[10]

It remains to be seen whether, after 200 years, this essential 'intimate knowledge' can be obtained from means other than the census. For now, at least, it seems that the census will continue. Whatever method is chosen, today's family historians must hope that it will prove as useful to future genealogy as the Victorian and Edwardian censuses have been to us.

Appendix I

CENSUS RECORDS ONLINE

FamilySearch: **www.familysearch.org**
Ancestry: **www.ancestry.co.uk**, Findmypast: **www.findmypast.co.uk**
TheGenealogist: **www.thegenealogist.co.uk**
British Origins: **www.origins.net**
FreeCEN: **www.freecen.org.uk**
Genes Reunited: **www.genesreunited.com**
Genuki: **www.genuki.org.uk**
TNA: **www.nationalarchives.gov.uk**
UK Census Online: **www.ukcensusonline.com**
1901 Census Online: **www.1901censusonline.com**
1911 Census.co.uk: **www.1911census.co.uk**
ScotlandsPeople: **www.scotlandspeople.gov.uk**
Irish Census Online: **www.census.nationalarchives.ie**
Online Parish Clerks: **www.onlineparishclerks.org.uk**
   Cornwall OPC: **www.cornwall-opc.org/index.htm**
   Devon OPC: **http://genuki.cs.ncl.ac.uk/DEV/OPCproject.html**
   Dorset OPC: **www.opcdorset.org**
   Essex OPC: **http://essex-opc.org.uk**
   Hampshire OPC: **www.knightroots.co.uk/parishes.htm**
   Lancashire OPC: **www.lan-opc.org.uk**
   Somerset OPC: **http://wsom-opc.org.uk**
   Sussex OPC: **www.sussex-opc.org**
   Warwickshire OPC: **www.hunimex.com/warwick/opc/opc.html**
   Wiltshire OPC: **www.wiltshire-opc.org.uk**
   Yorkshire OPC: **www.yorkshire-opc.org.uk**
Census Helper: **www.census-helper.co.uk**
Scotland's Family Census page: **www.scotlandsfamily.com/censuses.htm**
Office of National Statistics (ONS) guide to the 1981 and 1991 censuses: **www.ons.gov.uk/ons/guide-method/census/1991-and-earlier-censuses/index.html**
ONS Introduction to the 2011 census for England and Wales: **www.ons.gov.uk/ons/guide-method/census/2011/index.html**
Scotland's Census 2011: **www.scotlandscensus.gov.uk/en**
Scotland's Census Results OnLine: **www.scrol.gov.uk/scrol/common/home.jsp**
Central Statistics Office of Ireland Census: **www.cso.ie/en/census/index.html**, Historical Census Reports (Ireland): **www.cso.ie/en/census/historicalreports**,

Northern Ireland Statistics and Research Agency census: **www.nisra. gov.uk/ Census**

Glasgow University Guide to the census: **www.gla.ac.uk/schools/social political/ research/economicsocialhistory/historymedicine/scottishwayofbirt handdeath/thecensus**

Great Britain Historical Geographical Information System (GBHGIS): **www. port.ac.uk/research/gbhgis**

Online Historical Population Reports Website (HISTPOP): **www.histpop.org** (online access to the complete British population reports for Britain and Ireland from 1801 to 1937)

1831 Census Database (Staffordshire University): **www.staffs.ac.uk/schools/ humanities_and_soc_sciences/census/cen1831.htm**

BBC Census Infograph: England and Wales 1911–2011: **www.bbc.co.uk/news/ uk-18854073**

Useful Resources

Access to Archives: **www.nationalarchives.gov.uk/a2a**

A Vision of Britain through Time: **www.visionofbritain.org.uk**

Guide to Census Reports (1977): **https://www.visionofbritain.org.uk/census/ Cen_Guide**

Historical Directories: **www.historicaldirectories.org**

Scottish Population Listings: **www.myainfolk.com/Resources_files/Scottish_ Population_Listings_Pre1841.pdf**

Statistical Accounts (Scotland): **http://edina.ac.uk/statacc**

Census, Hearth Tax & Trade Directories: **www.myfamilyancestors.co.uk/census**

The History of the Workhouse: **www.workhouses.org.uk**

Cyndi's List: **www.cyndislist.com/uk/census**

Online Resources

National Library of Scotland digital maps: **http://maps.nls.uk**

British Newspaper Archive: **www.britishnewspaperarchive.co.uk**

Gazettes Online (London, Belfast and Edinburgh): **www.gazettes-online.co.uk**

Internet Library of Early Journals: **www.bodley.ox.ac.uk/ilej/journals**

Manx National Heritage's Isle of Man newspapers: **www.imuseum.im**

National Library of Scotland 'The Word on the Street': **http://digital.nls.uk/ broadsides**

Nineteenth-century Serials Edition: **www.ncse.ac.uk**

Welsh Newspapers Online: **http://welshnewspapers.llgc.org.uk**

A full history of the census in Ireland can be read at: **www.census.national archives.ie/help/history.html**

Tracing ancestors who cannot be found on the census: **http://blog.national archives.gov.uk/blog/missing-from-the-census**

The National Archives Guide to the Census: **www.nationalarchives.gov.uk/ records/research-guides/census-returns.htm**

General Register Office for Scotland Census Guide: **www.gro-scotland. gov.uk/ census**

Specimen forms for censuses 1971–2011 can be downloaded at: **www.census. ac.uk/goides/Qf.aspx**

Appendix II

CENSUS DATES

Tuesday, 10 March 1801
Monday, 27 May 1811
Monday, 28 May 1821
Monday, 30 May 1831
Sunday, 6 June 1841
Sunday, 30 March 1851
Sunday, 7 April 1861
Sunday, 2 April 1871
Sunday, 3 April 1881
Sunday, 5 April 1891
Sunday, 31 March 1901
Sunday, 2 April 1911
Sunday, 19 June 1921
Sunday, 26 April 1931
Friday, 29 September 1939 (survey for the national identity card)
Sunday, 8 April 1951
Sunday, 23 April 1961
Sunday, 25 April 1971
Sunday, 5 April 1981
Sunday, 21 April 1991
Sunday, 29 April 2001
Sunday, 27 March 2011

Appendix III

REGISTRARS GENERAL

Registrars General of England and Wales

1836–42	Thomas Henry Lister (1800–42)
1842–79	George Graham (1801–88)
1879–1900	Brydges Henniker (1835–1906)
1900–1902	Reginald McLeod (1847–1935)
1902–1909	William Cospatrick Dunbar (1844–1931)
1909–20	Bernard Mallett (1859–1932)
1920–45	Sylvanus Percival Vivian (1880–1958)

Registrars General of Ireland

1844–76	William Donnelly (1805–79)
1876–79	William Malachi Burke (1819–79)
1879–1900	Dr Thomas Wrigley Grimshaw (1839–1900)
1900–1909	Robert Edwin Matheson (1845–1926)
1909–26	Sir William John Thompson (1861–1926)

Registrars General of Scotland

1854–80	William Pitt Dundas (1801–83)
1881–1909	Stair Agnew (1831–1916)
1909–19	James Patten McDougall (1849–1919)
1921–30	Dr James Craufurd Dunlop (1865–1944)
1930–37	Andrew Froude (1876–1945)
1937–48	James Gray Kyd (1882–1968)

Appendix IV

ARCHIVES

The British Library
96 Euston Road
London
NW1 2DB
Tel: 01937 546060
www.bl.uk

Genealogical Office
2 Kildare Street
Dublin
County Dublin 2
Republic Of Ireland
Tel: 00 353 1 6030311
Fax: 00 353 1 6621062

General Register Office for Scotland (GROS) (now part of the National Records
of Scotland)
Ladywell Road
Edinburgh
Scotland
EH12 7TF
Tel: 0131 334 0380
https://www.nrscotland.gov.uk

Imperial War Museum
Lambeth Road
London
SE1 6HZ
Tel: 020 7416 5342
www.iwm.org.uk

Library and Archives Canada
395 Wellington St
Ottawa
ON K1A 0N4
Canada
www.collectionscanada.gc.ca

LSE Archives (William Farr's Papers) Archives Services Group Library
London School of Economics and Political Science
10 Portugal Street
London
WC2A 2HD
Tel: 020 7955 7223
Email: Document@lse.ac.uk
https://info.lse.ac.uk/staff/divisions/Risk-and-Compliance-Unit/LSE-Archives

Military Archives
Cathal Brugha Barracks
Rathmines
Dublin 6
Tel: 00 353 1 8046457
Email: militartarchives@defenceforces.ie
http://www.militaryarchives.ie/home

Mitchell Library
North St
Glasgow
G3 7DN
Tel: 0141 287 2999
https://www.glasgowlife.org.uk/libraries/venues/the-mitchell-library

National Archives of Ireland
Bishop Street
Dublin 8
Ireland
www.nationalarchives.ie

Parliamentary Archives
Houses of Parliament
London
SW1A 0PW
Tel: 020 7219 3074
E-mail: archives@parliament.uk
www.parliament.uk/business/publications/parliamentary-archives

Public Record Office of Northern Ireland (PRONI)
2 Titanic Boulevard
Titanic Quarter
Belfast
BT3 9HQ
Northern Ireland
Tel: 028 90 534 800
www.proni.gov.uk

Representative Church Body Library
Braemor Park
Churchtown
Dublin County

Dublin 14
Republic Of Ireland
Tel: 00 353 1 492 3979
https://www.ireland.anglican.org/

Scotland's People Centre (includes the National Archives Scotland, now the
National Records of Scotland)
HM General Register House
2 Princes Street
Edinburgh
EH1 3YY
Tel: 0131 314 4300
https://www.nrscotland.gov.uk/research/visit-us/scotlandspeople-centre

Society of Genealogists
14 Charterhouse Buildings
Goswell Road
London
EC1M 7BA
Tel: 020 7251 8799
www.sog.org.uk

The National Archives
Kew
Richmond
Surrey
TW9 4DU
Tel: 020 8876 3444
www.nationalarchives.gov.uk

West Sussex Record Office
3 Orchard Street
Chichester
West Sussex
PO19 1DD
Tel: 01243 753600
www.westsussex.gov.uk/leisure/record_office_and_archives.aspx

Staffordshire Record Office
Eastgate Street
Stafford
England
ST16 2LZ
https://www.staffordshire.gov.uk/Heritage-and-archives/homepage.aspx

GLOSSARY OF TERMS FOUND IN THE CENSUSES

A more comprehensive glossary of terms can be found at **www.census- helper. co.uk/census-abbreviations**.

/	Marks the end of a household
//	Marks the end of a dwelling or building
Ag. Lab.	Agricultural labourer (1841–81) may include all farming servants and labourers in husbandry (1841)
Ap.	Apprentice (1841–61)
Army	Members of HM land forces of whatever rank (1841)
Cl.	Clerk (1841–61)
DA	Daughter
Frmr	Farmer 'only the occupier of the land' (1851)
F. S.	Female servant (1841)
GD	Granddaughter
GS	Grandson
HD	Head
H. P.	Members of HM armed forces on half-pay (1841)
Ind.	Independent – people living on their own means (1841)
J.	Journeyman (1841)
Labourer	'to be described according to the place and nature of employment' (1851)
Lgr	Lodger 'pays rent … for any distinct floor or apartment'
M.	Manufacturer (1841)
M.	Married (1891)
m.	Maker – usually used with other words, such as 'nail m.' for nail maker
M. S.	Male servant
Messenger	'to be described according to the place and nature of employment' (1851)
Navy	Members of HM naval forces, including Marines, of whatever rank
NC	Niece
NP	Nephew

Occupier	'either resident owner or any person who pays rent' (1851)
P.	Pensioner in HM armed forces
Porter	'to be described according to the place and nature of employment' (1851)
Rail. Lab.	Railway labourer
S.	Single (1891)
SCH	Scholar 'children above 5 years of age, if daily attending school, or receiving regular tuition under a master or governess at home' (1851)
Serv.	Servant 'to be described according to the place and nature of employment' (1851)
Sh.	Shopman
Sis.	Sister
SL or SOLW	Son-in-law
SO	Son
SV or Ser	Servant 'to be described according to the place and nature of employment' (1851)
Tenant	'pays rent … for the whole of the house' (1851)
U	Unmarried
WI	Wife
Wid.	Widow (1891)

Appendix VI

ABBREVIATIONS

CEB:	Census Enumerators' Book
FHS:	Family History Society
GRO:	General Register Office
GROS:	General Register Office for Scotland
HISTPOP:	Online Historical Populations Report
LDS:	Church of Jesus Christ of Latter-Day Saints
LGB:	Local Government Board
NAI:	National Archives of Ireland
NAS:	National Archives of Scotland
ONS:	Office for National Statistics
OPC:	Online Parish Clerk
OPR:	Old Parochial Register
PRONI:	Public Record Office of Northern Ireland
RD:	Registration District
RN:	Royal Navy
RSD:	Rural Sanitary District
TNA:	The National Archives
USD:	Urban Sanitary District

BIBLIOGRAPHY AND
FURTHER READING

Hansard's Parliamentary Debates

Register of towns indexed by streets for the 1841–1881 census of England and Wales (LDS)

Family History Library Catalog (number 6026692)

Allison, K.J., 'An Elizabethan Village Census', *Bulletin of the Institute of Historical Research* 36 (1963), pp.91–103

Annal, David, *Using Census Returns, Pocket Guides to Family History* (Public Record Office, 2002)

Atkinson, Diane, *The Suffragettes in Pictures* (History Press, 2010)

Bisset-Smith, George Tulloch, *Vital Registration: A Manual of the Law and Practice Concerning the Registration of Births, Deaths, and Marriages. Registration Acts for Scotland, with Relative Notes on Vaccination and the Census, Forms, and Tables of Fees, &c.* (William Green & Sons, 1902)

Blomefield, Francis and Charles Parkin, *An Essay Towards a Topographical History of the County of Norfolk,* 11 vols (Fersfield, 1739–75)

Booth, Charles, *Life and Labour of the People in London,* 3rd ed. (Macmillan, 1902–03)

Booth, Charles, 'Occupations of the people of the United Kingdom, 1801–1881', *Journal of the Statistical Society,* XLIX (1886)

Chadwick, Edwin, *Report on the Sanitary Condition of the Labouring Population* (Home Office, 1843)

Chapman, Colin R., *Growth of British Education and its Records* (Lochin Publishing, 1992)

Chapman, Colin R., *Pre-1841 Censuses and Population Listings in the British Isles,* 4th ed. (Lochin Publishing, 1994)

Christian, Peter and Annal, David, *Census: The Expert Guide* (TNA, 2008)

Cohen, S., 'Anti-Semitism, immigration controls and the welfare state', *Critical Social Policy,* vol. 5, no. 13 (June 1985), pp.73–92

Cory, Kathleen B., *Tracing Your Scottish Ancestry* (Polygon, 1999)

Crawford, E. Margaret, *Counting the People: A Survey of the Irish Censuses, 1813–1911* (Four Courts Press, 2003)

Cruikshank, George, *George Cruikshank's Omnibus* (Tilt & Bogue, 1841)

Cullen, M.J., 'The 1887 Survey of the London Working Class', *International Review of Social History,* vol. 20, issue 1, pp.48–60

Drake, Michael, 'The Census, 1801–1891' in E.A. Wrigley (ed.), *Nineteenth Century Society: Essays in the Use of Quantitative Methods for the Study of Social Data* (Cambridge University Press, 1972)

Dyer, A. And Palliser, D.M., *The Diocesan Population Returns for 1563 and 1603*, 'Records of Social and Economic History' series (Oxford University Press, 2005)

Eden, Frederick Morton, *An Estimate of the Number of Inhabitants in Great Britain and Ireland* (Wright, 1818)

Erickson, Charlotte (ed.), *Emigration from Europe 1815–1914* (Adam and Charles Black, 1976)

Eyler, John M., 'Farr, William (1807–1883)', *Oxford Dictionary of National Biography* (Oxford University Press, 2004), **www.oxforddnb.com/view/article/9185**

Ffolliott, R., 'Irish Census Returns and Census Substitutes', in D.F. Begley, *Irish Genealogy: A Record-Finder* (Heraldic Artists Ltd, 1987)

Fletcher, David, 'The territorial foundations of the early nineteenth-century census in England' in *Historical Research*, vol. 81, no. 211 (February 2008)

Fowler, Simon, *Digging Deeper* (History Press, 2012)

Fowler, Simon, *Tracing Your Army Ancestors*, 2nd ed. (Pen & Sword, 2013)

Gatley, David Alan, *A User Guide to the 1861 Census and Vital Registration Data Base* (Staffordshire University, 1996)

Gibson, Jeremy and Medlycott, Mervyn, *Local Census Listings 1522–1930: Holdings in the British Isles* (FFHS, 2001)

Glass, D.V., *Numbering the People: The Eighteenth-Century Population Controversy and the Development of Census and Vital Statistics in Britain* (Saxon House, 1973)

Glass, D.V. (ed.), *The Population Controversy: A Collective Reprint of Material Concerning the Eighteenth-Century Controversy on the Trend of Population in England and Wales* (Gregg International Publishers Ltd, 1973)

Gordon, Major W. Evans, 'Royal Commission on Alien Immigration' (BPP, 1903), X, pp.451–60, reproduced in Charlotte Erickson (ed.), *Emigration from Europe 1815–1914* (Adam and Charles Black, 1976)

Hanson, John, *How to Get the Best from the 1911 Census* (Society of Genealogists, 2009)

Herber, Mark D., *Ancestral Trails: The Complete Guide to British Genealogy and Family History* (Genealogical Publishing Co., 1998)

Higgs, Edward, *Life, Death and Statistics: Civil Registration, Censuses and the Work of the General Register Office, 1837–1952* (Local Population Studies, 2004)

Higgs, Edward, *Making Sense of the Census: The Manuscript Returns for England and Wales, 1801–1901* (HMSO, 1989)

Higgs, E., 'Women, Occupations and Work in the Nineteenth-century Censuses', *History Workshop Journal* 23 (1987), pp.59–80

Johnson, G., *Census Records for Scottish Families*, 2nd ed. (Scottish Association of Family History Societies, 1997)

Kennett, Debbie, *The Surname Handbook: A Guide to Family Name Research Mapping in the 21st Century* (History Press, 2013)

Kitson Clark, G., *The Making of Victorian England* (Harvard University Press, 1962), pp.147–205

Lawson, G., *1861 Census Index Horsforth* (Wharfedale Family History Group, 1998)

Levitan, Kathrin, *A Cultural History of the British Census: Envisioning the Multitude in the Nineteenth Century* (Palgrave Studies in Cultural & Intellectual History, 2011)

Liddington, Jill, *Rebel Girls: Their Fight for the Vote* (Virago, 2006)

Mackenzie, Eneas, *A Descriptive and Historical Account of the Town and County of Newcastle upon Tyne: Including the Borough of Gateshead* (1827)

Mayhew, Henry, *London Labour and the London Poor* (G. Woodfall & Son, 1851)

Medlycott, Mervyn, 'Local Census Listings', *Genealogists' Magazine*, vol. 23, no. 8 (December 1990), pp.281–4

Neocleous, Mark, *Imagining the State* (McGraw-Hill International, 2003)

Newman, Dennis, 'The Census of Population', *Journal of the Royal Statistical Society. Series D (The Statistician)*, vol. 20, no. 2 (June 1971), pp.3–14

Nicholson, Juliet, *The Perfect Summer: Dancing into Shadow in 1911* (John Murray, 2006)

Parkinson, Elizabeth, 'Interpreting the Compton Census Returns of 1676 for the Diocese of Llandaff', *Local Population Studies 60* (Spring 1998), pp.48, 57

Paton, Chris, *Tracing Your Irish Family History on the Internet* (Pen & Sword, 2013)

Pender, Seamus (ed.), *A Census of Ireland, circa 1659: With Essential Materials from the Poll Money Ordinances 1660–1661* (Irish Manuscripts Commission, 2002)

Raymond, Stuart A., *Census 1801–1911: A Guide for the Internet Era* (Family History Partnership, 2009)

Rowlands, John and Rowlands, Sheila (eds), *Welsh Family History: A Guide to Research* (FFHS, 1998)

Sainty, M.R. and Johnson, K.A. (eds), *New South Wales: Census ... November 1828* (Library of Australian History, 1980)

Schürer, Kevin, 'The 1891 census and local population studies', *Local Population Studies* 47 (1991), pp.16–29

Stafford, Ann (pseud.), *A Match to Fire the Thames* (Hodder and Stoughton, 1961)

Stedman Jones, Gareth, *Outcast London* (Clarendon Press, 1971)

Steel, D.J., 'Earlier Censuses – Parish Censuses', *The National Index of Parish Registers, Volume 1: Sources of Births, Marriages and Deaths before 1837*, part I (Society of Genealogists, 1968), pp.333–6

Sykes, Dr David Allen and Whitwam, Stephen David, *Huddersfield township census return A-Z index. 1841 Census. Huddersfield Township Mi-Re*, Part 7 of 10 (Huddersfield and District FHS, 1994)

Szreter, Simon, *Fertility, Class and Gender in Britain, 1860–1940* (Cambridge University Press, 2002)

Thane, Pat, *The Foundations of the Welfare State* (Longman, 1982)

Thorby, R.P. and Benjamin, B., 'The application of the electronic computer to the 1961 population census of Great Britain', *The Computer Journal* 5 (4) (1963), pp.264–70

Wall, Richard, Woollard, Matthew and Moring, Beatrice, *Census Schedules and Listings, 1801–1831: An Introduction and Guide* (University of Essex, 2004), **www.essex.ac.uk/history/Staff_Research/working-papers/MW-RW-BM.pdf**

Waterfield, Henry, *Memorandum on the Census of British India 1871–72* (Eyre and Spottiswoode, 1875)

White, Jerry, *London in the 19th Century* (Vintage, 2008)

Whiteman, Anne (ed.) (with Mary Clapinson), *The Compton Census of 1676: A Critical Edition*, n.s. 10 (British Academy: Records of Social and Economic History, 1986)

Wright, S.J., 'A Guide to Easter Books and related parish listings', parts 1 and 2, *Local Population Studies*, 42 and 43 (spring and autumn 1989)

Newspapers and Periodicals

Bury and Norwich Post, and Suffolk Herald

Caledonian Mercury (Edinburgh, Scotland), Friday, 22 June 1860, issue 22071

Contemporary Review

English Woman's Journal (issues 1858–1864 online at **www.ncse.ac.uk**)

Family Links 1 (6), September 1982, and 1 (7), January 1983

Household Words

Illustrated London News (some copies online at **TheGenealogist**)

Irish Ancestor, 9 (2), 1977

Journal of the Statistical Society of London

Leader (issues 1850–1860 online at **www.ncse.ac.uk**)

Manchester Guardian

Monthly Repository (1806–1837) and *Unitarian Chronicle* (1832–1833) (online at **www.ncse.ac.uk**)

Northern Star and Leeds General Advertiser (issues for 1837–52 online at **www.ncse.ac.uk**)

Penny Illustrated Paper (1861–1913)

Proceedings of the Statistical Society of London, 1834–1839

Publishers' Circular (issues 1880–1890 online at **www.ncse.ac.uk**)

Quarterly Review

Survey Gazetteer of the British Isles

Survey of London (digitized by English Heritage, online at **https://www.british-history.ac.uk/search/series/survey-london)**

The Times (London)

Tomahawk (issues 1867–1870 online at **www.ncse.ac.uk**)

Victoria County History of the Counties of England

NOTES

Chapter 1

1. It has been suggested that Jesus was born earlier than ad 0, possibly in 5, 6 or 7 BC.
2. Elizabeth Parkinson, 'Interpreting the Compton Census Returns of 1676 for the Diocese of Llandaff' in *Local Population Studies* 60 (Spring 1998), pp.48–57.
3. Mark Neocleous, *Imagining the State* (McGraw-Hill International, 2003), p.56.
4. Kathrin Levitan, *A Cultural History of the British Census: Envisioning the Multitude in the Nineteenth Century* (Palgrave Studies in Cultural and Intellectual History, 2011).
5. D.V. Glass, *Numbering the People: The Eighteenth-Century Population Controversy and the Development of Census and Vital Statistics in Britain* (Saxon House, 1973), p.106.
6. 1801 (140) *Abstract, presented to the House of Commons, of the answers and returns made to the Population Act of 41st Geo. III. &c.*
7. Chris Paton, *Tracing Your Irish Family History on the Internet* (Pen & Sword, 2013), Chapter 3.
8. **www.histpop.org/ohpr/servlet/AssociatedView?path=Browse&active= yes&mno=2038 &assoctitle=Census%20%28Ireland%29%20Act,%201812& assocpagelabel=**
9. The Statistical Society of London became the Royal Statistical Society by a Royal Charter of 1887.
10. Missing ancestors are examined in detail in this TNA blog post by Audrey Collins: **http://blog.nationalarchives.gov.uk/blog/missing-from-the-census/**

Chapter 2

1. Seamus Pender (ed.), *A Census of Ireland, circa 1659: With Essential Materials From the Poll Money Ordinances 1660–1661* (Irish Manuscripts Commission, 2002).
2. Kathrin Levitan, *A Cultural History of the British Census: Envisioning the Multitude in the Nineteenth Century* (Palgrave Studies in Cultural and Intellectual History, 2011).

Chapter 3

1. Edwin Chadwick, *Report from the Poor Law Commissioners on an Inquiry into the Sanitary Condition of the Labouring Population of Great Britain* (Home Office, 184), pp.369–72.

2. Lister's works include *Granby* (1826), *Herbert Lacy* (1828), *Epicharis, an historical tragedy* (1829) and *Arlington* (1832).
3. www.histpop.org/ohpr/servlet/AssociatedView?path=Browse&active =yes&mno=2133&assoctitle=Census%20of%20Ireland,%201841&assocpage label=
4. Edward Higgs, *Making Sense of the Census Revisited* (University of London, 2005), Appendix 2, p.169.
5. Currency converter:1270–2017, http://www.nationalarchives.gov.uk/currency-converter/
6. *The Leicester Chronicle, or, Commercial and Agricultural Advertiser* (Leicester, England), Saturday, 19 June 1841, issue 1595.
7. George Cruikshank, *George Cruikshank's Omnibus* (Tilt & Bogue, 1841), p.72.
8. *The Standard* (London, England), Saturday, 12 June 1841, p.4, issue 5299.
9. *The Standard* (London, England), Friday, 2 July 1841, p.6, issue 21984. *19th Century British Library Newspapers: Part II.*
10. Gibson and Medlycott, *Local Census Listings 1522–1930* (FFHS, 2001).
11. *Household Narrative*, 185, p.1.

Chapter 4
1. GRO reference: deaths June quarter 1842, Westminster, vol. 1, p.329.
2. *The Essex Standard, and General Advertiser for the Eastern Counties* (Colchester, England), Friday, 13 September 1850, issue 1030. 19th Century British Library Newspapers: Part II.
3. Jerry White, *London in the 19th Century* (Vintage, 2008), p.134.
4. *Household Narrative*, 1851, p.164.
5. *The Times* (London, England), Thursday, 20 March 1851, p.5, issue 20754.
6. *The Times* (London, England), Saturday, 29 March 1851, p.4, issue 20762.
7. Charles Booth, 'Occupations of the People of the United Kingdom, 1801–1881', *Journal of the Statistical Society of London*, vol. 49, no. 2, 1886.
8. Higgs, *Making Sense of the Census Revisited*, p.14.
9. *Ibid*, p.170.
10. G. Kitson Clark, *The Making of Victorian England* (Harvard University Press, 1962), pp.147–205.
11. Full details on Chris Paton's discovery can be read on his blog: http://walkingineternity.blogspot.co.uk/2013/05/1851-religious-census-of-scotland.html.
12. www.open.ac.uk/Arts/building-on-history-project/resource-guide/source-guides/religious-censuses.htm.
13. *The Times* (London, England), Monday, 7 April 1851, p.5, issue 20769.
14. *The Times* (London, England), Wednesday, 9 April 1851, p.8, issue 20771.
15. 1851 Census, Form no 13: Circular to the Clergy of the Established Church (in the form of a letter by George Graham, the Registrar General), p.41.

Chapter 5
1. *Hansard*, House of Lords Deb 17 February 1854, vol. 130, cc. 783–816.
2. *Caledonian Mercury* (Edinburgh, Scotland), Friday, 22 June 1860, issue 22071.
3. David Alan Gatley, *A User Guide to the 1861 Census and Vital Registration Data Base* (Staffordshire University, 1996).
4. http://homepages.gold.ac.uk/genuki/MDX/census.html#census1861.
5. www.gla.ac.uk/schools/socialpolitical/research/economicsocialhistory/ history medicine/scottishwayofbirthanddeath/thecensus.

6. *Bury and Norwich Post, and Suffolk Herald* (Bury St Edmunds, England), Tuesday, 2 April 1861, issue 4110. 19th Century British Library Newspapers: Part II.

Chapter 6

1. *The Bradford Observer* (Bradford, England), Friday, 3 February 1871, p.4, issue 2531. 19th Century British Library Newspapers: Part II.
2. Higgs, *Making Sense of the Census Revisited*, pp.16–17.
3. *Census of England and Wales, 1871, Vol. IV: General Report*, p.vii.
4. Useful finding aids for this and other British censuses can be found through the Cyndi's List webpage **www.cyndislist.com/uk/census**.
5. *Hampshire Advertiser* (Southampton, England), Wednesday, 12 April 1871, p.4, issue 2590. 19th Century British Library Newspapers: Part II.
6. **http://www.hunimex.com/warwick/census/1871_enum_inst.html**

Chapter 7

1. 'Metropolitan Asylums Board', *The Times* (London, England), Monday, 4 April 1881, p.6, issue 30159.
2. *The Times* (London, England), Monday, 4 April 1881, p.9, issue 30159.
3. Higgs, *Making Sense of the Census Revisited*, pp.82–3.
4. Reference RG11/551/14, p.20.
5. A thorough investigation of surname-mapping and more details on researching surnames can be found in Debbie Kennett's *The Surname Handbook: A Guide to Family Name Research Mapping in the 21st Century* (History Press, 2013).

Chapter 8

1. *Hampshire Advertiser*, Wednesday, 4 March 1891, p.2, issue 4667.
2. 'Gales and Snowstorms', *Daily News* (London, England), Tuesday, 10 March 1891, issue 14018.
3. *Western Mail*, Thursday, 12 March 1891, issue 6806.
4. 'Gales and Snowstorms', *Daily News* (London, England), Tuesday, 10 March 1891, issue 14018.
5. Edward Higgs, 'Ad Hoc Censuses' available online at **http://www.histpop.org /ohpr/servlet/View?path=Browse/Essays%20%28by%20kind%29& active=yes&mno=2120**.
6. Similar changes affected parliamentary constituencies following the Redistribution of Seats Act of 1884.
7. 'The Census', *The Times* (London, England), 5 March 1891, p.3.
8. Charles Booth, 'Occupations of the people of the United Kingdom, 1801–1881', *Journal of the Statistical Society* XLIX (1886).
9. **www.oxfordhistory.org.uk/census/index.html**.
10. Report of Major W. Evans Gordon, *Royal Commission on Alien Immigration* (BPP, 1903), X, pp.451–60, reproduced in Charlotte Erickson (ed.), *Emigration from Europe 1815–1914* (Adam and Charles Black, 1976).
11. *Census of England and Wales, 1891, Preliminary Report*, p.1.
12. Kevin Schürer, 'The 1891 census and local population studies', *Local Population Studies* 47 (1991), p.25.
13. *Ibid.*, p.27.
14. *Census of England and Wales, 1891, Vol. IV: General Report*, pp.81–2: 'Explanatory Letter of the Registrar General of England and Wales Relative to the Census of 1891.'

Chapter 9

1. *The Times* (London, England), Saturday, 28 March 1896, p.16, issue 34850.
2. *Census for England and Wales, 1901, Preliminary Report*, p.2.
3. Reginald McLeod was knighted in 1905.
4. Higgs, *Making Sense of the Census*, p.17.
5. Booth's wife Mary recounted some of his experiences in Mary Booth, *Charles Booth: A Memoir* (Macmillan, 1918).
6. Charles Booth's London website; Notebook b347; URL: **https://booth. lse.ac.uk/notebooks/b347#?c=0&m=0&s=0&cv=0&z=-16.7229%2C0%2 C2503.4457%2C1489**

Chapter 10

1. *The Times* (London, England), Saturday, 27 May 1911, p.10, issue 39596.
2. S. Cohen, 'Anti-Semitism, immigration controls and the welfare state', *Critical Social Policy* (June 1985), vol. 5, no. 13, pp.73–92.
3. Higgs, *Making Sense of the Census Revisited*, pp.129–55.
4. Simon Fowler, *Tracing Your Army Ancestors* (Pen & Sword, 2nd ed., 2013), n.p.
5. Census reference RG14 – PN5440 RD87 SD3 ED5 SN147.
6. Census reference RG14 – PN5270 RD81 SD2 ED24 SN121.
7. Fuller details of the suffragettes' boycott can be found in Jill Liddington, *Rebel Girls: Their Fight for the Vote* (Virago, 2006) and Diane Atkinson, *The Suffragettes in Pictures* (History Press, 2010).
8. *Penny Illustrated Paper* (London, England), Saturday, 25 February 1911, p.240, issue 2596.
9. *The Times* (London, England), Saturday, 27 May 1911, p.10, issue 39596.

Chapter 11

1. Interview with Pete Benton, director of population and policy operations at the Office for National Statistics, Rosemary Collins, *Who Do You Think You Are?* Magazine, 26 March 2019, URL: **http://www.whodoyou thinkyouaremagazine.com/news/when-will-1921-census-be-available**
2. *The Times* (London, England), Monday, 24 November 1919, p.11, issue 42265.
3. *The Times* (London, England), Monday, 18 September 1939, p.6, issue 48413.
4. 'General Register Office: National Registration: 1939 Register'; The National Archives website URL: **https://discovery.nationalarchives.gov.uk/details/r/ C14663902**

Chapter 12

1. R.P. Thorby and B. Benjamin, 'The application of the electronic computer to the 1961 population census of Great Britain', *The Computer Journal* 5 (4), (1963), p.265.
2. Dennis Newman, 'The Census of Population', *Journal of the Royal Statistical Society. Series D (The Statistician)* 20 (2), (June 1971), pp.3–14.
3. *The Times* (London, England), Saturday, 28 April 2001, p.25, issue 67125.
4. Higgs, *Making Sense of the Census Revisited*.
5. **www.westminster.gov.uk/workspace/assets/publications/2011-Census-Why-Westminster-wil-1285775755.pdf**; **https://www.westminster.gov.uk/ sites/default/files/uploads/workspace/assets/publications/Enumeration-Challenges-in-Westmin-1285770412.pdf**
6. Parliament home page; Parliamentary business; Publications and Records; Hansard; Commons Debates; Commons Debates by date; Commons

Debates – previous sessions; Bound Volume Hansard – Debate; URL: **https://publications.parliament.uk/pa/cm200102/cmhansrd/vo010712/ debtext/10712-34.htm**

7. *The Times* (London, England), Monday, 4 April 1881, p.9, issue 30159.
8. 'Census 2011: can we do without it?' the *Guardian*; URL: **www.guardian. co.uk/news/datablog/2011/mar/25/census-jedi-pirate**
9. **www.bbc.co.uk/news/uk-politics-19669695**
10. Glass, *Numbering the People*, p.106.

INDEX